A Child of the Home Front

Joy Shellard

Natula Publications

First published in 2009 by Natula Publications
Natula Ltd, Christchurch, Dorset BH23 1JD

ISBN 9781897887745

A CIP catalogue record of this book is available from the
British Library.

Printed by Berforts, Stevenage, Hertfordshire.

Illustrations:
Pages 20, 21, 29, 34, 35 and 36
Courtesy of *The Bournemouth Echo*.

Other illustrations from the author's or publisher's collections.

Front cover: Joy Shellard at the age of 11.
Back cover: The Gardens at the rear of the Russell Cotes
            Museum and Art Gallery.

For my husband and my daughter

Acknowledgements

Mr and Mrs Simon Lilley for expert help and advice to a computer illiterate.

Mr Branski of Colour Copier, Highcliffe for skilled photocopying of ancient photos.

My memory bank for faithful (I hope) production of my experiences.

Garden Party with the French Soldiers from Dunkirk
Photographed using the Dufaycolor process
One of few colour photographs taken during the war

Preface

Why the Home Front? There are two reasons. As is well known, everyone living in the United Kingdom and not in the armed forces but yet enduring the dangers and privations of war and doing one's bit to win the war, was considered to be part of the Home Front. The further suitability of the use of 'Home Front' appertained to the locality.

As a child, during the war, I lived in the delightful town of Bournemouth and when there were threats of invasion, we were directly situated in the area where the Germans were most likely to invade. In fact, after the German blitzkrieg through Holland, Belgium and France, the South Coast became an area of restriction where it was difficult to obtain entry but very easy to leave and the population diminished rapidly; needless to say, there were no holidaymakers to swell the population in the summer.

Furthermore, my father worked and we all lived on the cliff top surrounded by hotels which were soon deserted and then commandeered by the armed forces. For a time we seemed to be the only living beings occupying the cliff top until the overseas air force boys and the American soldiers began to occupy the former luxurious hotels such as the famous Royal Bath, the Carlton, the White Hermitage and Marsham Court, to name but a few.

Memories are strange bedfellows and I have found that I remember most strongly the events of my childhood; maybe that time seems to pass more slowly as a child and that is possibly why the memories are so vivid. In addition, I think that the stirring emotions and outright differences that the war provided made all events and routines stand out more starkly. As a consequence, I am able to produce this book. Naturally, I also have some hazy remembrances but these I have not included in case there might be some inaccuracies.

Memories do not arrange themselves in chronological order but wherever possible I have attempted to give some idea of timing. Although not a specialist of the history of the war, I am able to do this because, like most families during the war, we all gathered round the radio each night at 9 o'clock to hear the BBC News.

Finally, as a server of words, I would like to say as a waiter might say, "enjoy!"

The Lull before the Storm

I was eleven years old and living in the ground floor flat of the Russell Cotes Museum, Bournemouth, as my father was the Curator. It was August 30th 1939 and 'no' I had not had cheese for supper or an over-sized meal. As was the custom, I went to bed at 8 o'clock, a happy child with no premonition of the terrifying nightmare I was about to experience. That horrible night I dreamed of bombs falling, great craters, fires and enemy planes.

Next day when I woke up, I told my family that war was about to be declared. I described my nightmare but was assured that Chamberlain had secured peace and that we had a pact with Russia. Only a madman would risk a war with the power of both Eastern and Western Europe against him.

Well Hitler was a madman and the next day he marched into Poland and we knew that Britain had, quite rightly, to fulfil its promise to the Polish people. But Russia had forgotten her verbal pact with Britain and joined with Germany in despoiling Poland.

A few days later, Chamberlain announced that Britain was at war with Germany. It was not the only time that I was to have premonitions in my dreams.

The next week, I felt that I was a child in limbo. We visited the Westover Ice Rink, which had been our rendezvous most of the summer holidays and were dismayed to learn that the Polish Ice Skating Champion and her sister who were practising at the ice rink were returning at once to their home country and, we never heard what happened to them.

The ice rink was almost deserted - no laughter and games, just a subdued hush. I personally had a feeling of immediate impending doom. I even had a guilt complex because I had been the fairy who brought in the New Year at the ice rink.

Within a few days, we heard that the Ice Rink was to shut at once because it had a glass roof. Then we had a notification from our school on Boscombe cliff that it was being evacuated to Highcliffe, a village nine miles east of Bournemouth.

St George's School which was evacuated to Highcliffe

Our parents discussed very seriously the idea of sending my two sisters and me to Canada. Amongst some families, this had seemed a good idea but the general exodus of the young generation was halted by the torpedoing of a large liner with its cargo load of children by a German U-boat in mid Atlantic.

My parents had already decided that it was best for a family to face dangers together but they were not hiding their heads in the sand. My father made elaborate efforts to provide a bomb shelter for us. The Russell Cotes Museum was originally a private mansion that had been built into the cliff and at the back of the building were some cellars cut out of the sandstone and well below ground level.

To one of these underground dungeon-like rooms, my father fitted a massively strong door to make the small dank chamber completely airtight. Then he made a large hole in the wall to the next cellar; this was over one foot square and probably more than one foot deep as the walls were quite thick in this part of the house. Into this hole, he placed a massive iron pipe to which he attached a hand-operated pump. The idea was to stave off a gas attack by placing a wet blanket in the pipe and sucking non-polluted air into the room by means of the pump.

Father thought of everything including supplies of tinned food and bottled water. This cellar seemed to me like an evil tomb from which there might not be any escape, but fortunately, we never had to use it.

My father was not the only person preparing air raid shelters. There were two recognised shelters: the Anderson which fitted into a hole made in the garden and the Morrison which was placed under a strong table or something similar in the house.

However, there were some most industrious people who made their own underground shelters from scratch. Such a person was Mr. Newman, my Aunt's secretary; he constructed the most elaborate one in my Aunt's garden in Tuckton Road, Southbourne and I did have occasion to use it once. I was playing tennis with a friend on my Aunt's tennis court and my friend's father had instructed us that we must go into a shelter if the siren sounded and he threatened that if we didn't obey he would 'knock our blocks off'.

I later discovered that this was a common phrase of his but at the time it seemed rather horrific, so we duly complied with his order and ran into the shelter a stone's throw away from the tennis court. Now, this shelter was comparatively luxurious and contained two beds and a sitting area, books, magazines and food supplies presenting the feeling of a pleasant little underground cabin and so we spent quite a comfortable half hour there, and I never discovered what it felt like to have my head knocked off.

Another fear that I anticipated was that of wearing a gas mask and fortunately, again, I never experienced it. When we went to collect our gas masks, we were supposed to have them fitted and somehow or other I managed to avoid this. This phobia was probably created when, at a quite young age, I had to have a tooth taken out using gas and I remembered the suffocating feeling I felt when I had the mask fitted over my face.

****

The 'phoney war' continued and my parents were increasingly concerned about our education as there was no junior school close by. The feeling of togetherness in these worrying times bolstered the whole family and this prompted my mother into engaging a governess. She chose a young lady with the sunniest of dispositions and our daily contact with her and the fact that nothing actually seemed to be happening around us allowed our spirits to revive.

4

There had been only one air raid warning and, if I remember rightly, this was the same day that Britain declared war on Germany – nothing happened and it was found to be a false alarm.

My father, knowing how we missed our skating and very aware that growing girls required plenty of exercise and more than our daily half hour walk before lessons began, came up with the following 'bright idea'. He reckoned that there would be quite a number of winter days when frost could produce approximately half an inch of ice, so he suggested removing the gravel off a sizeable terrace in the garden and then spreading a layer of clay over the whole area. Finally, the gravel would be replaced and the whole heavily rolled. When flooded the water would hopefully remain on the surface and even a short frost would provide a small skating rink.

It was a mammoth task and the whole family set to with a will. Apart from digging, carting and rolling, the main task of my sister and I was to be the collection of clay. Before post war stabilisation of the cliffs, clay collected in the gullies at the bottom of the cliffs in quite large quantities and this sticky stuff we collected in pails and brought home. The task was accomplished before the frosts came and that winter, like many of the winters at that time, there were numerous cold nights. We had a great time executing spins, jumps and spirals on the ice without any fear of falling through. However, the small size limited our activities so if the frost lasted for three or more consecutive nights we set out on our bicycles to Hurn, about 8 miles away, where the heath was always flooded in the winter. In the vicinity of the Ringwood spur road we gyrated and leapt about to our hearts content with other enthusiastic skaters.

Sometimes there were even enough of us to play ice hockey with walking sticks that we had thoughtfully strapped on to our bikes. I particularly enjoyed this because the excitement and exertion warmed my limbs and particularly my feet. Being the

Ice skating on the terrace

Ice skating at Hurn

smallest and lightest in the group, I was the guinea pig who had to test the thickness of the ice and consequently frequently ended up with saturated boots and frozen feet. I argued, in vain, that the heaviest should try out the ice first! A game of ice hockey did much to stir the blood! Sometimes we lit a small bonfire to thaw out our numb hands and feet whilst we sat around drinking our barely warm soup. On occasions, we managed to lumber over on our bikes a portable but large hand wound gramophone and were able to perform our waltzes and foxtrots to music. Rarely, we were able to cadge a lift in a commercial traveller's car. Such people were able to obtain petrol, as they were 'essential users'. I was not altogether in favour of these trips because, as the smallest member of the party, the seat usually reserved for me was a boy's lap and, since I had received no sex education, I spent the next few days worrying that I might be pregnant.

One of the minor difficulties of our education was ensuring that we had enough activity in the open air. Our governess was a good tennis player and fortune shone on us; as winter turned into spring and Hitler's forces became more active, the guests of the neighbouring hotels fled as did their owners to places far away from the English Channel. The owners of one nearby hotel, the Miramar, asked my father if he would look after their red shale tennis court and book it out to a small but regular clientele of local players. In return we would be allowed free and priority bookings. This suited the family very well and we quite enjoyed the duties of rolling, sweeping and watering and, of course, the daily games of tennis were a much appreciated bonus, particularly as we met the regular customers and intermingling with them gave us variety of play.

****

By now, the main infringement of our way of life was the increasing scarcity of some foods. The enemy had not as yet attacked our shores but his fleet of U-boats was waging an Atlantic battle in which our merchant shipping was so vulnerable – vital arms and ammunition were not getting through and all imported food was in extremely short supply. Britain had in the years between the two world wars, become increasingly dependent on foreign food and restoring our agriculture could not be an overnight miracle.

Having much in common with monkeys, we children greatly missed nuts. My father discovered a pet shop at Pokesdown, which sold peanuts for bird fodder, and having consulted my mother, I was sent on my bike to purchase a considerable quantity of these nuts. Imagine our dismay when we discovered that there were small bits of stone, maggots and other impurities in this bird food, so my task was not finished. I had to spread what seemed like endless quantities of peanuts out in batches on newspapers and carefully select the nuts that I thought were suitable for human consumption. I was not the least bit popular with the family if a small but juicy grub found its way into someone's mouth – my protestations that it was good protein were to no avail.

Yet another minor disaster occurred when my mother, looking through a food catalogue, noted that Christmas puddings were for sale. Appreciating that her own Christmas puddings well laced with brandy would probably only last one more year and anticipating that the war would probably last somewhat longer, she decided to order approximately 20 of these advertised 'puds'. Imagine our horror when it became time to open one of these Christmas delights and we discovered a mouldy concoction in colours of blue, green and gold. The puddings had been expensive but there was nothing to be done as the supplier had vanished out of sight.

My mother liked to present the family with home-made

9

cakes but eggs were in short supply and dried eggs had not as yet come on the market, so to supplement the family's greedy demand for cakes, especially if we had visitors, I had to pedal my way up to Westbourne extremely early on a Saturday morning. I enjoyed my Saturday lie-in so it was particularly difficult for me to obtain the first position in the queue in order to have the whole choice of goodies arrayed before me. It seemed to me that some people had been queuing all night. I always seemed to be in a position wedged between large and tall women and men and hardly being able to see the most popular cakes rapidly disappearing.

Due to my small stature, those behind me frequently dismissed me as non-existent and I was far too shy to say anything. We had all by this time learnt the rules of the queue and I sometimes got so annoyed after being by-passed by a number of people that I squawked out my order for some of the few remaining cakes and actually managed to get served. It seemed a question of survival of the largest. I absolutely hated this Saturday trek but there was some satisfaction when the whole family enjoyed tucking into the goodies, unless I was only able to produce rock cakes and not chocolate cream cake or Battenberg.

You may wonder why I had to travel about 4 miles to procure a few cakes; as my mother had always made her own cakes, she was not a regular customer at any bakery and many of the niceties of the food world which were not rationed were kept 'under the counter' for regular customers. The Westbourne shop was an exception and the stock was all sold out by 10 in the morning and the staff could go home.

On another occasion, I was forced to endure, deservedly so, the vigorous criticism of my family. I was accustomed to doing a little bit of cooking under my mother's supervisory eye and one day, somehow or another, we had obtained a packet of ground almonds. I pleaded with my mother for permission to make a Bakewell tart. All the cooking ingredients were stored in uniform glass jars on the side dresser but none of these jars was labelled, as my mother was most precise about their positioning; she obviously knew her way around her tidy shelves.

The Bakewell tart to my pride and joy looked quite the part and smelt wonderful when I took it out of the oven – the month's ration of eggs had raised the filling to a superb height and the correct gentle brown diffused the whole surface evenly. We sat down with delight to enjoy this piping hot treat, but the moment I sunk my teeth into the mouth-watering luxury, I thought my days were numbered. I had carefully weighed out and sifted into the mixture 4 ounces of salt instead of caster sugar. I must say that the family took it well and did not skin me alive and even waded through their portions of baked salt saying that if one considered it a savoury it could be endured in very small mouthfuls and believe it or not the whole of that tart was devoured! War conditions meant that it was a sin to waste good food even if it was messed up by little sister.

My mother had always been considered a good cook and with ingenuity and imagination she excelled herself with the meagre and varying rations. We enjoyed a whole new set of recipes; instead of nougat pudding, apricot soufflé and roast beef we had beetroot or carrot pudding, eggless cakes and soya bean casserole. Even the stale tea leaves left at the bottom of the teapot were used to make a fruit cake with cut apples substituted for sultanas and water taking the place of eggs. We had ice cream made from apple purée and dandelions and nasturtiums in salads. For breakfast, we had cooked cauliflower stumps with a sprinkling of very scarce cheese to make the dish palatable. We ate well but as I mentioned before, I was always hungry, but I think that we were fitter for it.

One of our favourite pastimes was trying to raid the larder without being detected. Our number one target was the peanut butter jar; this gooey thick substance was most amenable to standing up on its own and we were very successful at gouging out a large cavern in the centre without it being detected. My mother sometimes commented that the peanut butter didn't last very long but it wasn't on coupons and was not rationed, so when she could, she simply restocked.

One of my most enjoyable jobs was unloading the big box of groceries when it was delivered by an elderly man on a bike, who was beyond the 'call up' age. The items I unloaded always presented me with surprises. The rations excepted, which were always the same, the grocers and greengrocers supplied what they could and not what had been ordered. These substitutes rarely coincided with the items on my mother's list, which she had telephoned in the morning, and we were sometimes presented with items that we had never seen before such as whale meat (ugh) and spam (nice).

I remember an extremely unripe avocado pear turning up amongst the cabbages and I don't think that the greengrocer knew what it was but Mother was a good customer. When my mother discovered that it was listed on the bill as some sort of pear, she chopped the hard thing up with apples and some of her home bottled plums to make a fruit salad. Naturally, we all ate the fruit salad with our customary gusto but we declared that we really didn't think much of avocado pears. Another time my father produced some medlars and told us that they were supposed to be eaten when they were all mushy and seemingly bad and we didn't think much of them either but maybe they were riper than they were supposed to be!

Fresh fruit was only available for a few months in the summer apart from apples and pears which might keep up until Christmas and my parents were determined that we should all have some fruit in the winter (tinned fruit quickly vanished from the shops) so, in the months of June, July and August, home was turned into a bottling factory.

Father procured what was known as a fish kettle. It was so enormous that I think that it could have even cooked 'the fish that got away' and when it was placed on the gas stove it completely smothered it and even overlapped the sides. Most of the family was conscripted to work in the operation and my job was usually to prepare the fruit. As this activity was particularly time consuming, I took the fruit up on the roof, if the weather was pleasant, first checking that there was no one in the museum to notice my queer hand luggage and there I would spend hours topping and tailing gooseberries, de-stalking blackcurrants and red currants and peeling a few luxury peaches. I was happy as a sand boy gazing out to sea and consuming a berry or two every now and then, easing my conscience by the thought that they were too ripe to bottle.

When the bottles had been in the fish kettle in gently simmering water for a long time, they had to be taken out and the glass lids screwed on more tightly – this was a job for my elder sisters to do if our mother was out. Occasionally the seal was not adequate and when we came to open these bottles in mid-winter there would be a thick blanket of quite attractive mould on top. This we carefully removed in one operation and then we set to very cheerfully eating the contents, which seemed to have a most satisfactory taste. Possibly the fruit mould formed before the fruit had a chance to ferment, or perhaps we were all a little drunk without knowing it. Anyway, it didn't smell of wine and during these difficult times with no sell by dates we had to rely on our noses – if it smelt good, it was good.

Strangely enough, the war brought out a few goodies such as rose hip syrup, tinned blackcurrant puree and dried egg, which was excellent for making scrambled egg.

****

At this stage of the war, there were many activities in which civilians could contribute. In our garden wooden poles were substituted for iron hoops on which beautiful roses had luxuriated each summer. The metal was recycled for guns but we felt the garden looked more enchanting for the change and the roses did not object. But flowers were not essential for the war effort and my father was given *carte blanche* by the Bournemouth Corporation to change large areas of the garden into a mini market garden; this was beneficial for all parties. Only one gardener was supplied by the Council one day a week and my father joyfully took over most of the work. He dug up many of the rose beds and constructed one enormous strawberry bed. He planted rhubarb amongst the palms and blackcurrants and gooseberries between the peonies and the silver thistles. This supplied the aforementioned bottling factory.

Our demand for fresh salads was not neglected. Lettuces were planted in every available patch of soil between the perennial plants and tomatoes were nurtured in sunny sheltered spots. My father was so successful in protecting these tomatoes from the vagaries of the British weather and, by diligently covering the plants with items of worn out clothing on frosty nights, he was able to pick ripe tomatoes in January. The Bournemouth Echo declared this a record and sent round a photographer.

The soil in the garden was not very rich in nutrients and obviously required fertilisers which were not easy to come by. My father, needless to say, had an ingenious solution. The whole family was encouraged to use chamber pots or 'jerries' as they were sometimes called, a name that also appertained to our enemies but I doubt that there was any connection although, as children, we had a bit of a laugh about it. In the morning, these were lined up outside the back door and my father cheerfully took on the unenviable task of filling the watering can with this valuable liquid fertiliser and applying it to the earth round the fruit and vegetables. We had bumper, succulent crops but my mother was very careful to wash and wash the produce again and again.

During this lull before the storm - we had few illusions that all would end before Christmas, and my father prepared for the worst. There were many valuable pictures in the museum and art gallery and he appreciated that if the museum received a direct hit from a bomb they would all be lost so he worked out a distribution system whereby these works of art could be placed in churches in the surrounding countryside. The pictures had to remain under the umbrella of the museum's insurance policy so every placement had to be inspected by my father for suitability. This job required transport so my father bought a motor bike as being the most economical on petrol, for which he had to secure an essential user's permit. He toured the countryside looking for suitable accommodation for the pictures; any damp or excessive light in a church had to be avoided and of course, he had to obtain the vicar's consent.

This was an ongoing assignment as, when the pictures were in place, he had to every now and then check that all was well. However, this was not a chore to my parents as inspection provided a day out in the country, which was difficult for town dwellers in wartime owing to petrol shortage and difficult public transport. My mother loved these days out and happily mounted the pillion seat behind my father even though once she had come off the back when a dog chased the motor bike and she sustained a nasty injury to her knee.

We had regular school-time holidays from studies with our governess and during these breaks, I delighted in going on some of these expeditions. I remember one to Milton Abbas, which I believe was a type of convalescent and faith healing centre at the time. We wandered round the grounds and a series of unique grass steps greatly impressed me but the highlight of the visit was when I was presented with some deliciously ripe home-grown figs.

Some of my father's most enjoyable trips were to Air Force stations where the Victorian paintings sometimes hung incongruously on the mess walls. He loved these visits because in the First World War he had been in the Royal Naval Air Service and had been much involved with early flying of both balloons and aeroplanes. On one of these expeditions, I arrived on the motor bike with him and after considerable formalities was allowed into the camp.

As far as we were concerned, from the beginning of the war in September 1939 until May the following year the war was happening in a distant place; but all that was about to change.

The news was becoming more and more dismal, culminating with the British army and part of the French army being trapped by the German forces around Dunkirk. Then came the miracle of their evacuation which secured the safety of a considerable proportion of our brave soldiers and quite a number of our allies' men. Many of our local small and larger boats took part in this amazing operation including Bolsen's boats which, a short time before, had been taking happy holiday makers on trips round the bay from a small pier to the east of the main Bournemouth pier.

Bournemouth was now actively involved in the war both in sending boats to rescue British and French soldiers and as a centre to receive them. The horror of war was now all too obvious to us.

For propaganda purposes it was hailed as a victory but in our heart of hearts we knew that Britain was in mortal danger. True, it was wonderful to see photos in the papers of many of 'Our Boys' returning to our shores, but it was an army without any weapons.

The Storm

At this time, the news became more and more depressing and I recall a singularly grey day when the greyness was so intense that it seemed overwhelming. I don't know why, but on our early morning walk with our governess, as we approached the Bournemouth pier, I felt that the world was about to end and then we read on the placard outside the newsagent the dreaded headline 'PARIS HAS FALLEN'.

Our depression knew no relief, the impregnable Maginot Line which was to protect France and ourselves against the onslaught of Hitler's forces had been circumnavigated via Belgium and the lowlands of Northern France. Paris now lay at the mercy of Hitler and we knew by this time that mercy was not a word that operated amongst the German rulers. We no longer cheerfully sung *We're going to hang out the washing on the Siegfried line* or *Run Hitler, run Hitler, run, run, run*; matters were far too serious for such frivolity and we were full of foreboding as to what would happen next. We knew that our turn was next and that the full blitzkrieg would be directed at us. The coastal areas were to become a heavily fortified front line.

Everyone who could leave did so and no one was allowed to enter without a permit, but my father had to stay to guard the treasures of the museum and become a one-man fire fighting team cum air-raid warden.

Needless to say, we were extremely anxious to know what was happening and the B.B.C. was the great informer; naturally the News was heavily censored and propaganda was rife but we were not very aware of this and it became a daily ritual to listen to the B.B.C. News at 1 p.m. and 9 p.m. All activity ceased whilst we sat listening to the voices of Freddie Grisewood, Wilfred Pickles, Bruce Belfrage and John Snagge

17

to name but a few.

My mother almost had a panic attack when shortly before the B.B.C. News, the wireless stopped working. With great haste, I took the back off and pulled all the valves out and then put them back in exactly as they were and miracle of miracle the wireless worked! I earned many Brownie points that day.

Whenever Churchill broadcast to the nation we were held spellbound by his inspiring words and for many a day thereafter we would quote such phrases as "We will fight them on the beaches ..." and "Some chicken and some neck ..."

We never listened to Lord Haw Haw, the traitor who broadcast propaganda from Germany because we thought that it was unpatriotic, but some of our friends did and we laughed at his many threats but I am afraid that some of Haw Haw's dire predictions had a ring of truth in them. He sometimes named specific local areas that were to receive air raids. It seemed that this traitor to Britain had lived locally, some said in the area around Wimborne.

With a very real risk of invasion after the fall of France, Bournemouth took on the face of a town in siege. It was vital to stop the enemy landing on the beaches and so one of the first tasks was the dismantling of the two piers. Ironically, immediately prior to the war, Bournemouth Council had proposed the replacement of Bournemouth pier, which was considered in great danger of collapsing. When, in the interests of the war, it was decided to blow out a section of the pier near to the shore, high explosives at first were unable to achieve the objective and it was not until massive explosives were utilised that the pier yielded. However, this achievement was only secured by loss of glass from many local windows. The noise was horrendous and we would have been terrified if we had not been warned to stay indoors.

Another defence ingeniously devised was a tubular trellis with barbed wire entanglements, which resembled a wall of scaffolding extending all along the beach from Sandbanks to Hengistbury Head and behind this, mines were laid in the sand.

Naturally, no one was allowed on the beach, but much later in the war when the risk of invasion had receded, the mines were removed. There was a gash in the beach defences where a ship had foundered and the army made another small gap so that we were able to enter the water for a swim. It was quite a challenge to go out through the official entrance and swim along to the next gap about half a mile along. This many of us did repeatedly, but one day, my enthusiasm for this show of stamina was somewhat diminished. The tide was probably lower than usual and I found blood streaming down my legs and yet I had felt nothing. Running back to the official gap, the pain set in reinforced by the saltiness of the sea which, as a most efficient antiseptic, ensured that the nasty gash on my thigh healed up within a few days.

Pill Box at modern-day Highcliffe
This has fallen down the cliff since the end of the war

Beach Defences on Bournemouth Beach, 1946
Photograph courtesy of *The Bournemouth Echo*

Sunbathing on Bournemouth Beach amongst the defences, 1944
Showing the gap in the defences made for swimming.
Photograph courtesy of *The Bournemouth Echo*

There were many other defensive measures taken at this time when Britain had her back to the wall. Wherever the cliff dipped to sea level there were rows and rows of anti-tank blocks called dragon's teeth and concrete gun emplacements which were nicknamed pill boxes because some of them were round but they could come in all shapes and sizes, some carefully disguised to look like huts and others inserted in walls etc. Naturally, the pier approach at Bournemouth had rows of dragon's teeth.

In spite of all that was going on, we still managed to take our early morning walk with our governess along the promenade either to the East or to the West of the pier.

Walking with governess, Miss Vera Ford, on the promenade

One morning we were astonished to discover the promenade littered with huddled bodies; it looked as if all the tramps in the whole wide world had descended on this part of Bournemouth. As some of the bodies stirred in the early morning sun, we saw how miserable they were: wet, ragged, covered in mud and blue with cold. We urged our reluctant governess to speak to some of them and she soon discovered that they were French soldiers and that they had been transported from Dunkirk.

We returned home, our silence testifying to our feelings of compassion and then my sister had a bright idea. In childish extravagance, she asked, "Mummy can we invite the French Soldiers home for tea?" There were hundreds of them! Pragmatically my mother reduced their numbers to a manageable six, which was all our meagre rations would allow. What an invidious position to have to return to the 'huddled' masses and select six but, nevertheless, it was done, probably on the basis of those lying nearest and who were awake. Mark you, we had our qualms and worried what our parents would think when the sodden grimy guests appeared.

We waited with baited breath for 3 o'clock, the appointed hour. We were astonished when five immaculately presented French army gentlemen arrived as the clock chimed three. It was a beautifully sunny day in May, with all the climbing roses in bloom round their wooden poles and war seemed far away. We soon learnt through our governess interpreter and our feeble French conversation (blast those irregular verbs) that guest number six had reluctantly turned down our invitation because he had not managed to spruce himself up enough in his estimation, to go out to tea. We wanted to rush out and look for him but our duty was to entertain our new-found friends. Amazingly the conversation flowed largely through the expertise of our governess. We learned of family and loved ones back home. We saw many photos of babies, fiancées,

23

wives and pets and we even understood quaint anecdotes related in French. We laughed and laughed over the story of how one of our visitors in his supreme effort to tidy himself up for an English tea, had found his way to Bobbys (now Debenhams) and had asked where he could buy a 'comb'. His mispronunciation resulted in his being guided to the Ladies Underwear department where he was shown a variety of 'combinations'!

Garden Party with the French Soldiers from Dunkirk

At 4 o'clock, our mother brought out on to the rolling lawns of the Museum, a traditional English tea of sandwiches, home made scones and chocolate cake. Our eyes bulged; we hadn't seen such food since the beginning of rationing. Needless to say, we were on very short rations for the rest of the month living mainly off vegetables, but it was worth it to see the delight on the faces of our French friends. Naturally, we exchanged addresses, and in spite of the exigencies of war and the almost immediate return of these soldiers to the fighting in

France, we occasionally heard from one or two of them.

I often wonder what happened to these gallant gentlemen who were so anxious to uphold the honour of France at a traditional English tea-party and, "Thank you Mother for turning up trumps."

****

At this time, the Luftwaffe began to hurl its might at our small island. To begin with most of the German offensive was launched at the Royal Air Force, its aerodromes and planes in the air; Britain' s power in the air had to be destroyed before an invasion could take place. Both sides took enormous losses but our brave pilots had the edge on the Germans and Churchill was able to pronounce with his sonorous voice a victory in the air and the fact that, "Never, in the field of human conflict had so many owed so much to so few."

However, it must not be forgotten that the civilian factory workers toiled and toiled to produce the replacement planes and ammunition. Some adult friends of the family found themselves working in the Westover Garage in central Bournemouth on ammunitions – not only was the work extremely monotonous but it was dangerous to health. The workers had to drink copious amounts of milk which was supplied to them to avoid the effects of lead poisoning.

After the Luftwaffe's failure to annihilate the R.A.F., Hitler decided that he could win the war by destroying the morale of the British people through aerial bombing. In this destructive environment, there was much revenge and retaliation. Air Marshall 'Bomber' Harris was in charge of the massive Allied air campaign against Nazi Germany from 1942 until the end of the war; this 'saturation' bombing of German cities caused countless civilian loss of life and widespread damage. He was criticised quite heavily at a later date but at the time this was

WAR and the survival of the strongest.

I suppose mentally I was maturing because sometimes, and particularly at night, I had harrowing thoughts about not only English but also German mothers sorrowing for their lost sons killed in the war but we knew that we did not want to be under the yoke of the Germans and the only way to save life was to finish the dreadful war as soon as possible.

Tennis Party

In this war against civilians, Bournemouth received a not insignificant share of bombing. To begin with, we heard of incendiary bombs dropped on Hengistbury Head but this did not perturb us overmuch because the fires were quickly put out and we tended to be amused by the inaccuracy of the bombers. But then there was an explosive bomb dropped on a house in Crabton Close Road and some people were killed. This was closer to home and I remember going about my daily life in great fear but, with the resilience of youth, normality returned fairly quickly. There were lessons to be revised and a Junior School Certificate to be taken at a local school and there were meals to be anticipated and thoroughly appreciated – we were always ready to eat. There were still cycle rides, tennis and walks to exercise our bodies and to be enjoyed.

We also engaged in the excitement of watching through Father's telescope (which incidentally should have been given in to the authorities but Father was reluctant to do this as it had been a present from a dear friend) the dogfights over the bay. Oh the delight when a poor German plane met its doom but the anxiety and sorrow when one of our gallant spitfires or hurricanes was seen to fall out of the sky. In particular, we were horror struck when a spitfire was hit and came hurtling to the ground; it crashed near Leven Avenue near the Upper Pleasure Gardens killing its New Zealand pilot. The tragedy of it; a young man travelling from the other side of the globe to meet his death in a far off country. Later, I discovered that a very good friend, Mrs Eileen Hight, was related to this brave airman, Cecil Henry Hight. His grave is in the War Graves plot in the Cemetery in Gloucester Road, Boscombe.

We loved it when we saw parachutes opening up and gracefully descending because we knew that each time this happened a life was saved.

****

During this time, everyone was much encouraged to recognise the various aeroplanes we might see in our skies and this became an absorbing hobby for me. I filled many scrap books with pictures and silhouettes of planes culled from newspapers and magazines. Later on in the war when some Royal Observer Corps men were stationed in Bournemouth, while they were awaiting posting to various strategic points around the country, I was delighted to meet one of these young men. He was able to give me the latest aircraft silhouettes, some of which were still on the official secrets list. Naughty, naughty, when we were surrounded by posters shouting at us 'Careless talk costs lives' but then I was obviously serious about aircraft recognition and was determined to join the Royal Observer Corps when my call-up time came (the war was over before I reached the age of 18).

On a long walk from Bournemouth pier to Hengistbury Head and back, I remember discussing the feasibility of recognising German planes from English ones by the sound of their engines. Many people swore that they had the ability to make this distinction but in the early part of the war, we decided that it was probably an ability to distinguish between British fighters and German bombers. But could listeners tell whether they were hearing a marked difference between say a Messerschmitt 109 and a Spitfire which both had single engines. Needless to say, we came to no conclusion but we enjoyed the discussion and the long walk, even though it was somewhat marred by coastal defences.

It was not long before we were testing our knowledge of aircraft. Bournemouth, although not severely bombed had its share of raids. At one stage, these were mainly at night. Many of the siren alerts were after dark and they were caused by German bombers crossing our area to reach the industrial Midlands where factories were churning out aircraft and ammunition at amazing speed. At first, the sirens sounded late in the evening and the alert remained on until the planes returned in the small hours, at approximately 4 o'clock. Later the sirens were attuned to the immediate danger of planes passing overhead and so we would hear two separate alerts, one in the evening and one in the early morning, each lasting perhaps an hour or more as wave after wave of bombers passed overhead.

Bournemouth Gardens, 1942
Photograph courtesy of *The Bournemouth Echo*

The morning alert was the danger one for Bournemouth because some of the German bombers had not been able to drop their bombs over the target and so, unfortunately for us, they deposited their heavy weight on the coast in order to save fuel and the difficulty of landing with a dangerous load of explosives.

At the beginning of the night raids, my parents would wake us up and shunt us into camp beds in what my father considered was a safe part of the house and where he had erected the table tennis boards with a strong support to protect us in the event of the ceiling falling down. My mother did not like the idea of us sitting up all night long in the confined space of the cellar; she knew that our health would suffer as, nearly every night the German bombers passed overhead. Likewise, she did not think that her children would be fit if they slept every night in a rather stuffy part of the house in uncomfortable camp beds, so we returned to our pleasant rooms in the front part of the house for healthy nights' sleep. It must have been difficult for parents to weigh up the risks. Ours decided against having listless kids unable to do their studies and to enjoy themselves.

Later in the war in the winter of 1941, we were all assembled in our lounge ready for our evening walk along the cliff top in the dark; blackout was vigorously enforced at this time – no street lights and the few motorists who had to travel after dark had severely dimmed lights. However, we managed to achieve our nightly constitutionals without bumping into lampposts although I do remember sometimes stumbling over steps. Maybe it was because we had our share of a plentiful supply of compulsory carrots.

Anyway, I had secured the blackout round the house, which was one of my little tasks. The blackout in the lounge consisted of some boards with extremely heavy lined velvet curtains in front of them. Without any warning, just as we were all ready to step out of the front door, there was the most almighty explosion and the heavy blackout precautions hurled themselves half way across the floor. Fortunately, none of us was hurt and the angry splinters of glass were lying buried underneath the curtain. One might say, "Saved by a curtain."

When we explored the rest of the flat, we found shattered glass everywhere, ceilings collapsed and heavy glass fittings strewn over the floor. In fact, almost nowhere would we have been safe except in the small corner of our lounge. In our so-called safe sleeping area, the ceiling had collapsed; the table tennis boards and their strong supports had fallen on the flimsy camp beds and completely crushed them.

There was one other undamaged corner of the house, namely our dug out cellar prepared for a gas attack, with all its accoutrements including the large buckets for waste material!

We learnt the next day that a single German bomber had somehow eluded the radar warning system and dropped two parachute mines which carried an extra dose of explosives, one at the bottom of the cliff and one just out to sea. The cliff had ensured that the damage was limited to a certain extent.

My father was not able to examine the state of the museum and art gallery until daylight; it was far too dangerous to wander around with candles and it seemed almost impossible to get up either of the staircases.

In the morning he was met by a very sorry sight; the leaded glass roof had completely collapsed onto the hall below and our dear goldfish in the ornamental pond were dead. There was a litter of ceilings and glass everywhere but we were allowed only a small peep in case there might be some more collapsing.

Miraculously on further inspection, my father discovered that most of the treasures lay unharmed under the debris and even some of the glass cases were intact; I believe that a few pieces of valuable china had been broken in other cases not so well preserved.

We were extremely fortunate that the very next day all our windows in the flat were either re-glazed or boarded up. Most people whose property had bomb damage had to wait weeks to have their windows seen to, but in the case of the museum, there was a great risk of looting. Our experience of this particular raid reinforced a fatalistic attitude that all British people were developing, 'If your name was on the bomb there was nothing that you could do about it' and 'If you heard the whine of the bomb falling then you were safe'. I don't know if there was any scientific basis for this theory, but we all believed it. On the optimistic side, we just hoped that providence hadn't been busy with our names and we gradually learned the art of peaceful sleep.

****

Returning to the daylight raids, which somehow were not as terrifying as the ones in the dark, I remember one particularly well and being young and ignorant, I was saved from the trauma that I might otherwise have felt. It was a beautiful, sunny day, not a cloud in the sky. My father and I were peacefully picking from the abundant crop of luscious strawberries under a gigantic net that my father had erected to try and keep out the birds from eating the berries in the large round bed which in peacetime had luxuriated in roses. Suddenly my father shouted, "Take cover under the rhododendron bushes" and being a moderately obedient child, I did not stop to ask why.

The rhododendrons very close by formed a dense cover being rather special ones with large leaves and heavy blooms and they had been there many years. Crouching under the bushes, I saw them, Messerschmitt 109s, several of them flying only 30 or so feet above our hedges.

By coming in so low over the sea, the planes had eluded our radar beams and so there was no air raid warning. At the same moment that I saw the planes, I heard what sounded like extremely large hailstones hitting the leathery leaves around us.

My father must have been amazed when he heard me asking, "Is it hailing?" I don't know what my father replied because by then I realised that I was experiencing being machine gunned. On this occasion the Messerschmitt 109s continued on their way and killed and wounded a number of people in the Bournemouth Pleasure Gardens and ironically left bullet holes in the War Memorial by the Town Hall.

There were not so many bombs dropped in 1942 but May 23rd 1943 was a black day for Bournemouth. A low-level bombing raid occurred in the centre of town without any warning and it wasn't long before Beales was ablaze.

My father, gauging that the bombers would fly off very quickly, urged us to go up on the roof of the museum where we had a superb, almost aerial, view of the whole of Bournemouth. My mother was most reluctant to let us go and I must confess that my knees were knocking at the thought, but Father was insistent that this was a historic occasion and one that we should remember for the rest of our lives. Perched on our viewpoint we witnessed the devastation of many of our favourite haunts. Not only was Beales rapidly being completely gutted by fire from incendiary bombs but there was evidence of utter destruction at the Punshon Memorial Church and the adjoining Central Hotel, the Metropole Hotel at the Lansdowne, the Wests Cinema, Terrace Road and the Shamrock and Rambler Garage in Holdenhurst Road.

Between 1940 and 1943, there were many other bombs dropped, I understand, well over 2,000 in Bournemouth, but some really stand out in my memory. There was a disaster at Alma Road School when children were killed.

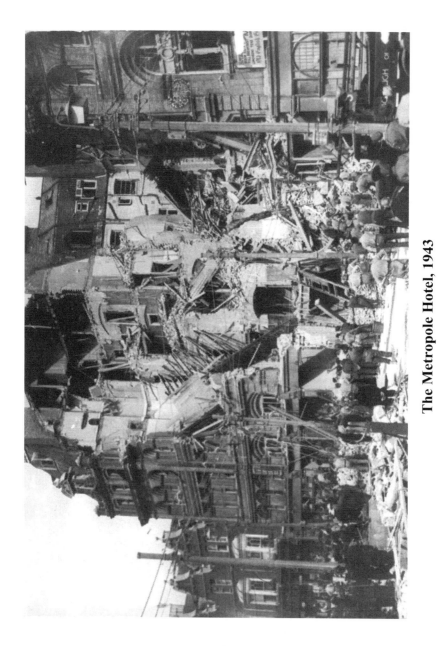

The Metropole Hotel, 1943
Photograph courtesy of *The Bournemouth Echo*

Beales Department Store, 1943
Photograph courtesy of *The Bournemouth Echo*

Beales Department Store, 1943

Photograph courtesy of *The Bournemouth Echo*

Woolworths, then in the square, was completely put out of circulation; this latter features in my memory bank because it was a favourite store for children and it was a real treat for my sister and I to visit this shop since there we could buy articles for six old pennies. In theory, nothing cost more than 6d in the shop but I remember when my sister bought a cactus plant she was dismayed to be charged one shilling: 6d for the plant and 6d for the pot, but it was worth the money because it bore many progeny which were spread around to friends all over Bournemouth.

There was a bomb up Bath Road and one in Parsonage Road, both of which were rather too close for comfort. Fortes in the Square was damaged and that meant the end of our trips, often in the blackout, to have an ersatz ice cream as our second course for supper.

The spire of St Andrews Church nearby was damaged and had to be removed. It was here that I attended church at a later date, and was inspired by the preacher, Dr Davidson, to keep smiling. Looking around, I saw how worried and miserable most people looked and of course, they had every reason to look that way but a smile might improve matters and I have been trying to smile when appropriate ever since.

Robert Louis Stevenson's house in Westbourne was destroyed. This was a house that we often passed on our walks round the chines in that area and as I had read *Kidnapped*, I liked to peer through the hedge and look at the house where the great man had lived.

****

One of the most moving experiences that I had was in 1940. Early in the year, my cousin, Dick Silvester, had been stationed at Wool in Dorset where the Royal Army Tank Corps had its headquarters and whenever he had time off he visited us and we grew very fond of him. Not only did he look extremely smart in his uniform but he was able to show us magic tricks with string.

Presently he was posted overseas and in accordance with the strict security of the war, we did not know where. Some little time later, I had one of my horrible nightmares in which I saw a massive tank battle in the desert and I saw with terror our dear cousin being killed. I suppose that I was so upset that I had to tell someone, so my mother heard all about the ghastly dream. In a little over a week, we heard the miserable news that our cousin had been killed in the desert in North Africa.

Our cousin Dick prior to his posting in North Africa

Her Majesty's Stationery Office produced well-illustrated publications with some pictures in colour and the first one I bought contained a picture replicating the grim nightmare that I had experienced. From that time, I bought every H.M.S.O.

booklet I could and read them avidly although I could not understand some of the technical information. I treasured these publications for many years after the war, but when I saw them deteriorating in the attic, I found a very worthy home for the collection at The Keep Military Museum at Dorchester.

We also looked forward to the weekly magazines of the *Picture Post* and *The Illustrated* both of which contained many pictures and these together with the B.B.C. 9 o'clock news were the main sources of our knowledge of the war. Mummy used to take the *Daily Mirror,* but this we were not allowed to read and Daddy took *The Times*, which we did not want to read.

Robert Stark before he was taken prisoner

Later on in the war, I had another dream which did not predict such a sad event. My sister had become very attached, as indeed we all had, to a young Northern Irish bomber airman called Robert Stark, awaiting posting in Bournemouth for quite a long time, but presently he took up his duties raiding targets in Germany and then one day my sister heard that he was 'missing presumed dead'. It was then that I recalled my dream that I had experienced some days previously in which I saw Robert Stark being taken prisoner by the Germans. Without a thought, I assured my sister that he was alive and a prisoner of war and this conviction was confirmed a few weeks later when we heard that he was alive and in one of the notorious Stalag Luft prisoner of war camps. He was released at the end of the war and recovered well from the rigours of the prison camp.

I was growing older and I understand that the prescience of dreams diminishes with age so I had no more alarming experiences in my sleep and, in fact, from that date to this, I have experienced hardly any dreams leave alone nightmares.

****

Was it the invasion or was it not? One Sunday in 1940, my sister, Paddy, and I went to our favourite church, St Andrews, in the Square for morning service. Spiritually refreshed by the excellent sermon delivered by Dr Davidson, we returned home with few worries on our minds. We were confronted at the bottom of our road, Russell Cotes Road, by a barricade and a group of soldiers who would not let us pass. We explained that we merely wished to return home but the officer in charge assured us that no one lived on the cliff top and all roads to there had been closed. We were adamant that the Russell Cotes Museum was our home but the military presumably thought we were a couple of cheeky kids having them on and there is no doubt that my sister was capable of such a trick. However, I think our faces told another story because we were becoming increasingly alarmed, fearing that perhaps our parents had been evacuated and so the officer consented to sending one of the soldiers to see if there were any inhabitants living in the Museum. My mother evidently answered our back door, which was in Russell Cotes Road, and assured the army that she was indeed expecting her two daughters back from church. So we were escorted by two soldiers to our home but we were warned that on no account should we go into our front garden and certainly not out on to the cliff top. We were also told that we must not look out of our windows.

Confined, as it were to barracks, curiosity consumed us and even overcame any scruples my father might have had but, of course, he himself had not received the warning, so out came the telescope with which he scanned the sea but there was nothing to be seen there. Because of the topography, it was impossible to view the beach and we knew that we would be in trouble if we sallied forth into the garden and from thence to the cliff top. We were still baffled by the mystery when the alarm was over and we were permitted to emerge from our enforced confinement.

At a much later date in the war, we heard from what we considered several reliable sources that the Germans had prepared themselves in their barges in the French ports across the English Channel and were about to set out or had actually done so, to invade the southern coast of England. The vigilant British Navy, following the time honoured tactics of Sir Francis Drake, set fire to the sea by pouring oil on the surface and then lighting it. The Bournemouth beaches and cliffs were shut because burned German corpses were being washed up on our shores. I believe that it has been authenticated that bodies were certainly coming ashore but where they had come from and who they were, has not been clearly established in my mind, so I still say, "Was it a failed invasion or was it not?"

In these times of strict censorship, many other rumours were rife and one much bandied about at the time concerned Brownsea Island in Poole Harbour. Here it was said that spies were transmitting information to the Germans.

Another story relating to Brownsea Island was certainly

true. The northern section of the island was used as a decoy for German bombers. Here fires were lit when Poole was in danger of being devastated and the enemy planes poured their bomb loads on this desolate part of the island and so Poole was saved from destruction.

****

But it was not all gloom and destruction; there were moments of great excitement and one I remember particularly well was when King George V1 and Queen Elizabeth visited the town to inspect the Canadian, Australian and New Zealand airmen who were stationed in Bournemouth prior to posting to various air stations. The visit was fairly 'hush hush' so there were no very great crowds lining the streets and waving flags. I suppose, because my father was a Council employee he knew about such things but only at the last minute and we hurried down Westover Road to the Regent Cinema's restaurant, which was opposite the Pavilion. Here we had an excellent view of the fountains and the surrounding area, which was filled with rank upon rank of airmen.

Presently the King and Queen arrived, the Queen looking so elegant and beautiful with such a winning smile for all the service personnel. I had never seen Their Majesties before and I was suitably thrilled but a little disappointed that the two princesses who were my heroines were not present.

I had a book, which I treasured, and which was profusely illustrated telling of the day-to-day lives of Princess Elizabeth and Princess Margaret and as they were about the age of my sisters and me, I was particularly drawn to them. This visit did much for our morale - to think that Their Majesties would visit our town when there was so much danger around. I recall vividly that our Royal family did sterling work in keeping up the spirits of the British people in their time of peril. They shared the dangers and the hardships that we all endured. They insisted on staying in Buckingham Palace and they were the first to visit bombed out citizens and bring them cheer. There was hardly a person in the land who didn't follow with almost personal interest their innumerable visits to bomb sites, stricken towns and the armed forces.

My sister Paddy, Miss Vera Ford and Paddy Woods

The King's speeches, somewhat haltingly delivered on Christmas Days, were listened to almost with reverence and he delivered many words of comfort to the British people. Who could forget his broadcasting of the famous quotation, "I said to the man who stood at the gate of the year, 'Give me a light that I may tread safely into the unknown' and he replied, 'Put your hand into the hand of God which is better than a light and safer than a known way'." These may not be the precise words of the quotation but it is as I remember it.

43

Life on the Home Front during the Storm

After three years under the excellent tutelage of our governess, Miss Vera Ford, during which time my sister, Paddy, and I both passed our Junior School Certificates, I began to get itchy feet. My eldest sister was at boarding school in Bristol, which, at the beginning of the war, was considered to be a fairly safe area since it was too far away from Germany for the aeroplanes, with the limited range of those times, to reach.

However, once Hitler's forces had over run France, the enemy planes were able to fly to most of the British Isles and the great cities of England became prime targets in Hitler's efforts to annihilate the morale of the British. Bristol along with cities such as Coventry, Bath, Southampton, Birmingham, Plymouth and, of course, London, suffered great devastation. My sister's school decided to evacuate from the centre of Bristol.

The Wills family of cigarette fame most kindly offered the school their beautiful home, or should I say mansion in the countryside outside Bristol and here the school flourished; the extensive grounds were much appreciated and in particular the fruit orchards where peaches might be found by the boarders. It was fortunate that the school did evacuate because the original school buildings were severely damaged.

Returning to my itchy feet, we learnt much from our charming governess but there were some subjects that I longed to know more about such as Algebra, Geometry, and Latin and, although my sister and I were great chums and never quarrelled, I longed for the fellowship of school. I had great difficulty in persuading my parents, because they could not understand why I wanted to learn Latin, Maths and Science – girls in their estimation grew up to become wives and mothers and had no need of such learning. However, I managed to prevail and my mother sought out a suitable school, namely Talbot Heath.

Talbot Heath School, the south front

I had to go for an interview and take a short examination and I knew as soon as I saw the attractive buildings and the grounds of heather and pines and the games field that, that was where I wanted to be, so naturally I made desperate efforts to be as nice as I possibly could. This proved very easy to accomplish as everyone was so kind, both teachers and pupils and even the Headmistress, Miss Stocks. Later, although the Head struck terror in our hearts if we misbehaved, I think we all admired her for her fairness, authority, organisation and inspiration. Well, I managed to get a place in the school and made many friends and several who have remained lifelong pals.

But the learning side was somewhat more fraught – as I had

never done any Algebra. Geometry and Latin and my form mates had been working at these subjects for at least two years, I was all at sea because I did not understand the fundamentals. For my first Geometry Examination, I obtained 15 out of 100 and my Algebra result was worse, just 5 and three of those were for neatness - quite simple to achieve when there was virtually nothing on the page.

I can't say I quickly caught up but over a three year period I managed to squeak through my examinations thanks in large part to my eldest sister's various boy friends who did my homework for me with a few explanations. Friends gathered round me when we had to give our Maths homework in and we all managed to do moderately well out of my sister's army friends.

However, this is personal and does not really have anything to do with the War but there were many aspects of the 'emergency' as it was sometimes called, which affected school life. Naturally we did have to take our gas masks everywhere with us; it was almost as important as having the correct books in class. We did miss quite a bit of schooling because of air raid warnings; in fact, the School Certificate that we all took when we were 15 or 16 was supposed to have been made easier because of wartime conditions, not that we noticed it.

This fact might have accounted for the nearly 100% pass rate that the school achieved in an examination where the candidate had to pass at least five subjects with compulsory English, Maths and a foreign language. Mark you, our teachers were good although somewhat elderly on the whole; the young graduates had joined the armed forces. Then, in addition, we had all originally passed an entrance exam. Some of our schooling was limited because we had an evacuated school with us.

Southampton town centre and port area had been completely obliterated (the fires could be seen from

Bournemouth about 30 miles away) and St Anne's School with its proximity to the centre was badly damaged, so its pupils used our school in the afternoon. It was most cleverly organised; we could not go to our classrooms in the afternoon because St Anne's pupils were using them but we were able to do all our sports and we could use the hall, gym and dining room if it was wet for country dancing. We were also able to use the music room for 'musical appreciation' and the art room, so it was a case of serious work in the morning and as far as I was concerned more enjoyable pursuits in the afternoon.

What was so amazing was that we never saw any of the Southampton students; it was as if they didn't exist, but we managed to become quite chummy with some of them. We used to leave little notes in our desks for the afternoon occupants and they would reply in the same manner.

A strange thing occurred; quite unexpectedly I caught chickenpox and was confined to home for three weeks, this being the quarantine time stipulated in those days. When I eventually returned to school the mystery was solved – it transpired that the girl using my desk had suffered from chickenpox and the germ had been transmitted to me through the desk, chickenpox being contagious. I wasn't complaining, I had had a nice holiday.

****

Much more disrupting to our scholastic studies were the air raids. We had well constructed air raid shelters in the grounds and when the alert siren sounded, we had to drop what we were doing instantly and march in single file to our allotted air raid shelter with no talking or running. We were not allowed to take anything with us except our gas masks and once seated on the benches in the shelters we had to remain in complete silence

47

until the All Clear sounded. This silence for me was agonising for my imagination ran riot with nightmarish thoughts. What if a bomb dropped actually on the shelter or nearby and we couldn't get out and so were entombed? What if an incendiary bomb dropped on the entrance and we were all burnt alive? Of course we could all appreciate why we had to obey silence – there were different forms in the one air raid shelter all doing different work and more important it was essential that if there was an emergency we could hear at once any commands the teachers might give and that gave me more food for alarming thoughts. Luckily, the siren alerts that I experienced at school did not last very long at this stage of the war most of the air raids occurred at night.

As regards lunches, the food was not bad, because the Ministry of Food deemed that it was important to feed the children well, but the school dining room was not of the best. Talbot Heath was built in 1936 and its building programme had been curtailed by the war so that the dining room was in temporary accommodation but it coped well for cooked meals and for packed lunches. I alternated between packed lunches, cycling home for lunch and school meals. One of my school friends sometimes cycled home with me and almost invariably on these occasions, quite by chance, we had herrings for lunch. The cycling there and back took at least half an hour, so, after we had removed all the tiny bones from the fish, it was panic eating to finish the meal and get back to school in time – talk about indigestion! Fish was not rationed although sometimes in short supply and my father was firmly convinced that herrings were good for growing children.

Sometimes a number of us used to pack picnics and cycle the short distance to Meyrick Park. This we were not supposed to do because the school needed to know that we were either in school for lunch or with our parents. Luckily, we did not get caught and we had great fun cycling up and down the bunkers on the golf course. We were careful not to ride over the greens and as far as my parents were concerned, they were quite happy about our picnicking.

Lunchtime in Meyrick Park

Another lunchtime escapade involved a British Restaurant; these restaurants were established during the war so that everyone could afford to have a simple but nourishing meal at a cost of one shilling (5p). To keep the cost down, these restaurants were self-service but the customer could have three courses and there was plenty of food. Mainly these restaurants were in halls but presently the well-known Luculus restaurant in the Pavilion opened its doors, at lunchtime only, to serve British Restaurant customers. In the evening, it reverted to its posh status, but we discovered that lunch, simple and wholesome was served by waiters in smart uniforms in quite plush surroundings. Sometimes a small gang of us would cycle down to the Pavilion and have one shilling's worth of luxury. We all found it a great giggle for a bunch of young school kids to have waiters running round after them. My parents knew all about it, but nevertheless I think we would have been expelled if the School had got wind of it.

****

Holidays were most impractical during the war, but whilst I was at school, I had what might be called a near holiday. Towards the end of the summer term and continuing into the holidays, Talbot Heath sent parties of its older pupils on harvesting trips. It was a time when farmers needed extra workers and older children were encouraged to help. We thought of it as a fun thing to do and at the same time, we considered it as a patriotic effort, which made it doubly desirable, particularly if we were lucky enough to be chosen for the term-time expedition.

At this time of the year, the main tasks were fruit picking and potato lifting and there was no shortage of volunteers. The trip that I went on took us to the delightful country town of Wickham. We took our bikes on the train to Fareham, from whence we cycled to Wickham. The roads were extremely quiet because only essential users were allowed petrol and, it was pretty country scenery.

When we reached our destination, we found that our accommodation consisted of two large huts, one for sleeping and the other was a dining room with very simple kitchen equipment one end; some canvas had been erected outside as a screen for when we washed in cold water from small basins and other necessities were serviced by chemical closets.

It was a strange life and not what town dwellers were accustomed to, but children adapt very quickly and we hardly noticed any discomfort and most of the time we enjoyed

School Party at Wickham

ourselves greatly. I was allocated to the fruit picking farm and I gather the allocation depended on size – larger youngsters went potato lifting, and as I was definitely one of the smallest ones in the group, my job was mainly blackcurrant harvesting. I was a wee bit disappointed because I considered myself tiny but strong and tough and then, too, most of my close friends were in the big and mighty group harvesting potatoes. I understood that the work in the potato fields was very wearing and a trial to backs whereas fruit picking became rather boring and somewhat back aching also as the bushes were kept deliberately low for ease of harvesting. We were given a few instructions on how to pick the currants and warned that if we did not do it correctly there would be no berries the next year. This worried me considerably so I picked extremely carefully and therefore did not achieve the results in pounds weighed that most of the others did. Then too, I rather liked blackcurrants and I am afraid that the very fat juicy ones did find their way into my mouth, but we had been instructed that we must not put very ripe fruit into the enormous baskets that we were given. I earned the dubious reputation of being the greatest consumer. It was assumed by the authorities that after a couple of days, we would not want to ever eat another blackcurrant, but somehow that psychology did not work with me.

We worked in pairs and my partner, after we had exhausted all we could possibly think of to say, which was naturally quite a lot, decided to sing all the popular songs of the day that we knew in order to avoid boredom setting in. We found that we knew quite a lot. I was amazed that my partner opted for such a distraction because, I could barely sing a note in tune, but fortunately she, herself, was not over musical and anyway I usually knew the words.

We would walk a few hundred yards into the centre of Wickham where some sort of truck picked us up and took us to

Staff at Wickham

Pals at Wickham

53

our destination and there we would work in the fruit fields all day with a break for lunch when we ate our packed lunches prepared by our teachers and an additional local lady who helped with the domestic chores and the cooking. All credit to our teachers who carried out a taxing task wonderfully well. Naturally, as kids we did not appreciate what they accomplished but with hindsight they did a marvellous job at looking after 30 youngsters and all that went with living in a rather primitive way of life that I am sure none of them were accustomed to.

Our lunches were somewhat samey and so we got into the habit of arriving at our pick up point a little early so that we could visit the bakery and buy a few extras such as meat pies – one square inch of meat, and a mass of potato all surrounded by rather thick and heavy pastry or some sort of bun. There wasn't much choice but we knew how hungry we would get by lunch time. It was while waiting in the queue, that I had a most memorably horrible experience. The lady in front of me went into a full epileptic fit. As I had never seen anything like it in civilised Bournemouth, I was truly scared, but the villagers took it in their stride and dealt with it quite casually as if it was an every day occurrence, which it might well have been.

Medical science was not as well developed in those days, particularly for poor people living in rural areas and we townies, unaccustomed to rural conditions, did not escape unscathed. One of our party went down with pneumonia and she was nursed by our gallant teachers in an area constructed between the two huts. We were not allowed to see her and we were so worried that she might die that her illness put a real damper on our spirits. We were asked to keep quiet when we were in the dining hut and so we talked in hushed whispers and only when necessary. Added to which, we knew that pneumonia was a most serious illness and this was before the days of antibiotics; penicillin was in its infancy and not in general use. Fortunately, she made a complete recovery and was able to go home at the end of our fortnight.

Another girl, who was a particular friend of mine, arrived home with rheumatic fever and we spent the rest of the school holidays visiting her in her sick bed. Fortunately, she too, made a quick and complete recovery. In a strange way, I had a kind of guilty feeling concerning her illness, all to do with the discovery of mushrooms in the next field to our camp. One morning, several of us waking early and having done our ablutions in cold water out of the bowls allotted to us, decided to go for a short walk before breakfast. We discovered that the field next to us was alive with wonderfully large mushrooms. We gathered as many of them as we could carry and took them to our teachers who were cooking our breakfast of interminable porridge. They were delighted and we were able to have delicious fried mushrooms added to our menu. So popular was this that we decided to get up early the next morning by the process of banging our heads on our pillows six times before we went to sleep which process worked quite satisfactorily as an alarm call for six o'clock. We dressed quietly and quickly, but when we clambered into the next field, we discovered that there was hardly a mushroom to be seen. It was obvious that someone had been out picking before us.

Next night we set our alarm clocks earlier by the same head banging method and were delighted to discover once more an abundance of mushrooms. This procedure continued, enabling us to gather mushrooms alternate days but by the end of our stay we were rising whilst it was almost dark and in addition the dew was so heavy that we were retuning from the rather long grass with soaking wet feet and feeling somewhat cold. I was rather concerned that our early morning forays had caused my friend's illness. Illness, however, was not limited to our harvest camp and there were cases of dysentery in one that was in North Dorset.

There were other holidays that I had during the war, but we had none as a family, because my father considered that it was his duty not to leave the museum unattended and although he went to London on business a number of times and managed to include some measure of entertainment for himself such as skating, he knew that the rest of the family was protecting the premises by simply being there.

My mother had no holiday at all throughout the war because she did not want to have one without the whole family, but, fortunately, she did love her home and considered it the best place in the world, which was not so far from the truth, so what was the point of leaving it. Added to which, travelling during the war was not at all easy.

The Wye Valley

However, my sister, Paddy, and I had two visits to the Forest of Dean and the Wye Valley at a cross between a summer school and a health farm. Here we had healthy food as per the Hay Diet, which basically meant that we ate largely fruit, vegetables and nuts and in addition the food was vegetarian but not vegan, so we did consume dairy food. I must say that we all enjoyed the food enormously and there was plenty of it because much of it did not rely on rationed food. Naturally, we had to hand in our ration books to the organisers. There were talks and discussions on healthy living and many dancing and exercise classes. We also had to help round the house and as I enjoyed cooking, I managed to worm my way into the kitchen for my duties, which consisted of preparing vegetables. No, we didn't peel potatoes, we just washed them and we shelled peas and sliced beans. But it was good to be around the cooking and see what was done with foods that I had not come across before, such as corn on the cob, cashew nuts and sandwiches with sweet fillings such as honey and dates and cashew nuts and honey – yum, yum.

Ross-on-Wye

57

Naturally, we had time to ourselves and my sister and I spent our time exploring the district on our bicycles. You may wonder how our bikes appeared, as it were, by magic. No, we had not cycled all the way from Bournemouth, but we had cycled a fair distance. First of all our parents saw us on the train at the West Station that no longer exists. From this station, one could travel to such places as Bristol and Birmingham, but we needed to get to the other side of the Severn, which meant going up to Gloucester. As the train we required started out from the West Station, it was fairly punctual, but during the war the time of arrival and of connections was an unknown quantity. Trains often stopped between stations if there were air raids and military trains and hospital trains in particular had priority.

On one of our journeys, I recall waiting whilst endless carriages of a hospital train went by and we felt greatly saddened at the thought of all the sick and mutilated boys in the seemingly endless train.

Chepstow Castle

Monmouth

Wye Valley and Forest of Dean Brochure Cover

To get to Gloucester we had to change at a small town miles away from anywhere it seemed and wait and wait which we did on this benighted platform getting more and more hungry as the minutes went by. It didn't help at all that facing us at one end of the station an enormous factory announced in huge letters that it was the home of Carsons Chocolates. After about one and a half hours, our train did appear and then we were on our way to Gloucester. The two fine bridges across the Severn near Bristol did not exist then. Once we reached Gloucester out came our bikes from the guard's van and we quickly found our route to the Forest of Dean – the travelling along the Bristol Channel valley was low lying and in war-time almost devoid of traffic. And so we had on our summer school the luxury of bikes to visit wonderful old towns such as Chepstow, Monmouth and Hereford. This area being on the border between England and Wales has an abundance of castles and the well-preserved ruins of castles such as Raglan, Monmouth, Chepstow and Goodrich intrigued me. I liked to imagine what they were like in their heyday and the way of living of the inhabitants.

There were also many beauty spots, one of the most beautiful ones being Symonds Yat which we had great difficulty in finding as we did not pronounce it the correct way when asking for directions; in fact we had great difficulty in understanding the local dialect which to our ears was distinctly Welsh; the only part of a sentence that we understood was the almost universal ending of "look you". On the whole we found our way around with a map and a pre-war guide book.

My sister and I had two of these holidays in the Forest of Dean and I must say that I enjoyed my second visit a few years later much more. At the time of the first visit, I felt quite out of place with a group of ladies past their teens, but on my second trip, I managed to fit in more easily.

I cannot recall the exact time, but sometime in the period between the Blitz and the arrival of the V bombs in 1944, when there was a lull in enemy action, my sister and I spent a fortnight at Richmond; we stayed with some people Daddy had met on one of his business trips to London. The house was almost opposite the Richmond Ice Rink which was on the other side of the River Thames and this was our daily destination where we revelled in the thrill of skating indoors on an ice rink where the ice was not spattered with reeds or bits of gravel coming to the surface and had not frozen in ripples. We were in elite company because this is where the champions trained under the watchful eye of Arnold Gerschwiler but they were a friendly group and found time to chat with us. Naturally we gave our ration books to the dear lady who was putting up with us but somehow she was not able to make such good use of our rations as our mother did and that together with the amount of exercise we were having caused considerable hunger pangs until we discovered a wonderful bakery only a short diversion from our route to the rink.

It was whilst we were staying here that unknown to us, we came across our first experience of Alzheimer's disease. We could not understand why our landlady's mother sat down to meals with us and immediately drew our attention to the beautiful view across the River Thames. We agreed most heartily with her and perhaps added another comment about the view and then once again she would draw our attention to the view and this continued throughout the meal. We couldn't understand why she didn't change the topic, but as she was a particularly charming old lady, we went along with the conversation trying to introduce new ideas which were never taken up.

****

I suppose I ought to consider my weekends spent on my aunt's small farm as holidays because they were most enjoyable and offered a change of scene. Call up for women commenced shortly after war was declared and month by month the age group became older and older until it reached the age that my aunt had attained, probably somewhere around the late forties. For someone like my aunt who liked her afternoon snooze, it would have been a great trauma to have joined the armed forces and nursing and factory work would have been almost as foreign to her way of life. However, work on the land was a reserved occupation and so Aunty Addy decided to buy a tiny farm in Arrowsmith Lane near to Canford School.

The farm or small holding consisted of approximately 10 acres; it had a small stream at the front with ducks and geese and then there was a small amount of arable land on which potatoes were growing. Further on there was a small but attractive bungalow and behind this dwelling was a field with a couple of cows and a goat and beyond that some pig sties and further on a large hen house. My aunt knew nothing about animal husbandry but her secretary cum chauffeur was a gentleman who could turn his hand to anything. Unfortunately he was not around at weekends and that was when the pigs got loose, a cow became poorly and the geese wandered off.

Next door was a large farm but it was a long way to go to find the farmer and ask for his help. So one by one the animals were sold off apart from the pigs and the hens which my aunt was just about able to cope with. The field was ploughed up and potatoes grown and a vegetable garden was planted. It was about this time that I was called in to help at weekends, My aunt would not go out at night because she hated the dark and in the country with the blackout the lanes were pitch dark so she found it extremely lonely; I was needed as a companion help. The pigs still got out on occasions but with tuition from

62

the friendly farmer neighbour we learnt how to round them up with much shouting and some hefty sticks which we used very gingerly. To reach the farm the only practical way was to cycle (how useful bikes were).

My route led me up to Wallisdown and then across Canford Heath which at that time was a most extensive wild area devoid of any habitations. Across the heath was an extremely rough gravel track which occasioned a few tumbles but my nightmare was a gypsy encampment in the middle of this desolate area. It wasn't too bad in daylight, but even then, I must admit that I peddled like mad with my heart in my mouth until I was out of sight. Come winter, when I would be crossing this barren heath at dusk or even in the dark immediately after school with just my feeble light for company (even bicycles had to have dimmed lights), the ride almost amounted to terrifying. The gypsies were probably quite pleasant people but they had a bad reputation at that time and I had witnessed their pushy ways down Westover Road trying to sell white heather.

However, I so loved my weekends at the farm, I was prepared to put up with the spooky ride. We would spend time in the outhouse boiling up the food for the hens and then over to the henhouse to feed them and collect the eggs. Then there was the vegetable garden to attend to and the pigs to have their swill. Meals were great with wonderfully fresh eggs and vegetables and of course, there was bacon. Farmers had to sell their produce in the market, in this case Wimborne, but they were allowed to keep some back for personal use. There was plenty of time left over the weekend for a good read, which my aunt enjoyed as much as I did; she loved reading detective stories and I discovered, delving into her library, Richmal Crompton's *Just William* books and their humour had me chuckling away. Luckily, my aunt had most or all of these books because each weekend I would read at least a couple of them. Unfortunately, I had to do my homework since I cycled back straight to school without going home first.

****

I think bicycles were absolutely essential to children with a busy life – public transport was poor and unreliable and cars were out of the question unless there was proof of essential use. Most car owners stored away their cars for the 'duration' and many took to their bikes. Even my mother, who had not ridden since she was a young child, bought a bike and very bravely seated herself on its saddle and wobbled her way around the garden until she had enough confidence to tackle the roads. Inevitably, the roads were almost devoid of traffic and once my mother was on the public highway there was no stopping her and as with so many other people it became a hobby.

Her favourite trip with my father was to Ringwood where there was an old world thatched tea place that served up jolly good teas; the tomato sandwiches were out of this world, so I often accompanied them. Part of the enjoyment of cycling was engendered by the lack of road signs and even road names, so that our trips out exploring became an orienteering sport. I remember well, one of these exploratory trips when cycling along a lane near Hurn which we did happen to know and being caught in a rain storm that quickly turned this road into a shallow flood, we suddenly spotted a new road of tremendous width that was so well constructed that it had no puddles on it. Although puzzled, we obviously migrated to this drier surface and speculated as to why it had been built; we travelled a considerable distance along its super smooth surface until it abruptly ended and we were forced to return to the muddy lane. We later learnt that this road was the runway for the new aerodrome of Hurn, which became operational shortly after.

Another pastime we took up was roller-skating. Our flat at the museum leant itself to this sport. There were two lengthy corridors with smooth concrete floors and even quite

64

considerable slopes so on wet days when we did not venture out we were allowed to roll up the coconut matting that normally covered these corridors and then race up and down them, spin and jump on basic roller skates clipped to our shoes. We sometimes took them out with us and if there wasn't anyone about we would skate down the steep hill to the pier and build up enormous speed all the time wondering if we would be able to stop. Sometimes we funked it and swerved into the wooden barrier that separated the Overcliff Promenade from the edge of the cliff and certainly, if we saw anyone coming, this is what we did, sometimes even hastily taking off our roller skates and hiding them. We seemed to know that we were not supposed to do this although there was nothing to say that we couldn't.

One windy wet winter day, we discovered one of the large shelters on the beach promenade empty; there was no one about and the concrete looked invitingly smooth. We had a wonderful time there until a beach attendant discovered us and gave us a right telling off.

Other fun pastimes we had, consisted of playing badminton and table tennis when the museum was shut; this occurred on Sundays and in summer after 6 p.m. In winter, as it was impossible to fully black out the museum, closing time was half an hour before dusk. The badminton took place in one of the art galleries and we used the centre picture screen as a net; it was a trifle high and of course, we couldn't see the shuttle till it arrived over the screen but this made the game even more hilarious. Naturally, we had to be very careful that no damage was done and so we wore appropriate shoes and stationed ourselves well away from any of the pictures. Table tennis was played on the long table in the dining room; we had to place a thick cloth over the immaculately polished table and then we placed the two table tennis boards on top. Again, we were very careful to ensure that we did not damage any of the valuable exhibits.

Our parents also adopted various pastimes and hobbies. I have already mentioned my mother's wobbly assays into cycling but apart from this, she found herself too much occupied with bringing up children and domestic chores to develop other hobbies. Help in the home virtually disappeared when war broke out and ours was a big place to run. My mother eventually found what was known as a daily but her hours of work were very limited. My mother made a great friend of her and my memory of this helper, is one of finding her ensconced in the kitchen having cups of tea and gossiping with my mother, but I imagine she must have done a certain amount of work. My mother loved to meet her friends for a morning cup of coffee and this she managed to continue but some of her friends were called up if they didn't have a family, so her social life was curtailed.

My father took up woodcarving and he decided that he wanted to chip out a bust of me from a large trunk of wood that someone had given him. I was to be represented looking up to the skies and the title of the piece was to be 'Spitfires'.

Mummy provided a challenge saying that Daddy could not possibly get a likeness, as, apart from some simple carpentry that he had done at school, he had no experience of carving. My father insisted that if he used callipers for measuring every aspect of my head and shoulders from the scientific standpoint he was bound to attain a likeness. I submitted to innumerable measurements at almost any time of the day. The argument continued for a lengthy time but finally when Father had finished the carving, I felt that he had achieved an excellent likeness, but I did not express an opinion because my mother still insisted that it was not like me. Apart from this new hobby, my father did not have the time to develop any new pursuits other than those connected with his work.

****

66

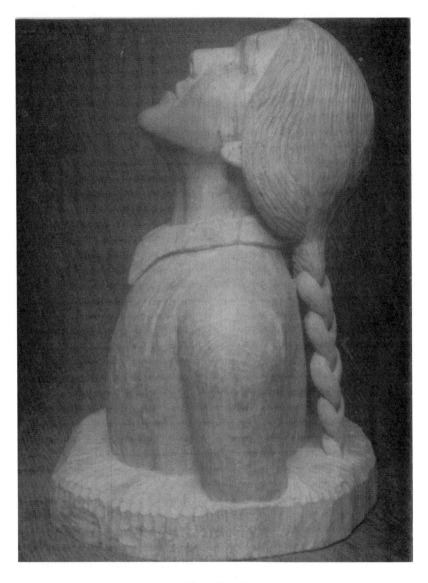

'Spitfires'

67

At the beginning of the war, there was a kind of hiatus whilst people wondered what was going to happen and then, if it was possible, it was 'business as usual' in defiance of what the enemy was doing. There was one innovation to which my father readily succumbed in his work. All across town, Red Cross shops opened; it was a time when people were disposing of some of their possessions because of war-induced upheavals and the most common articles to be thrown out were books and paintings, particularly Victorian ones, which were decidedly out of fashion. Now, the Russell Cotes Museum was a Victorian building with a largely Victorian collection and my father knew a considerable amount about Victorian paintings. These Red Cross shops were like the modern charity shops and people were pleased to contribute their no longer wanted items to them knowing that they were helping the war effort and in particular the wounded and prisoners of war. So father scoured these shops picking up for a few shillings quite valuable paintings for the museum collection and some, that were not suitable, to adorn our own walls.

Something else that was no longer wanted was old books and my father selected suitable books to give to me at Christmas. The excitement of waking up on Christmas morning and discovering that I could not move my feet because there were so many books littering the end of the bed, knew no bounds – mainly Henty, from whom I gained much historical knowledge, Dickens, Buchan and Ainsworth.

Throughout the war, my father continued organising art exhibitions: the Southbourne Art Society held its annual art exhibition; there were sculpture exhibitions and Contemporary Art ones, and these required much work because artists and collectors had to be approached and transport and insurance arranged, but my father was anxious to encourage living artists and particularly local ones. Because of his policy, Bournemouth saw many war works of art. I particularly remember a very fine sculpture illustrating Churchill's well-known phrase 'Blood, toil, tears and sweat' and then there was an equally fine painting demonstrating the foolishness of war depicting a jester surrounded by skulls burning money entitled 'Anno Domini 1940 as I See it'.

This picture really made me think, particularly as we were studying at school the war poets of the previous 1914 – 1918 war writing about the horror and futility of war, but more about this painting later.

From these exhibitions, the Museum gained some valuable additions to its collection, because the Museum and Library Committee usually gave permission to buy one or two items from each exhibition. Sometimes the works of art were selected by public acclaim. Visitors buying the catalogue and viewing the exhibition were invited to fill in a voting slip stating their favourite; this particularly applied to pictures selected to be included in the Picture Borrowing Scheme – an innovation of my father, which resembled the book libraries. We were sure that these borrowed pictures brought much joy into the sometimes rather bleak lives of war harassed local residents.

Another duty my father continued throughout the war was the issuing of a Russell Cotes Museum bulletin which was sent to other museums, many of them abroad. This publication unfortunately had to be somewhat curtailed in the number of issues per year because of paper shortages, but its high quality was still maintained.

****

I have frequently mentioned my hunger pangs but I haven't said anything about feeling cold in the winter. It wasn't bad in bed in spite of always having the window open – Father was a great believer in fresh air – because we had hot water bottles of the rubber variety to begin with. When these perished with age,

69

Blood, Sweat & Tears

Anno Domini 1940 as I see it

stone bottles were substituted since rubber was in extremely short supply. We also had eiderdowns (duvets had not as then been produced in the U.K.) which were rather heavy and then, of course, we had a number of blankets. On extremely cold nights we might scrounge another eiderdown; the resultant weight above us made it difficult to breathe if lying on one's back, so I always slept on my side, but at least we managed to keep warm.

Daytime was a different matter. Coal was in extremely short supply as so much was required for war manufactures and we were supposed to economise on electricity. Most people relied on one coal fire and possibly a boiler in the kitchen although back boilers were very popular which involved utilising some of the heat from the open fire to heat the water. There were electric fires which patriotic people and, of course, we were all patriotic except the spivs, were only used to warm a room whilst it was in use. As a consequence, most people shivered their way through harsh winters and there were a number of them during the War. Incidentally, spivs were people who took advantage of war conditions and shortages to make money and were considered almost equivalent to enemies within our midst.

We were, however, in a most fortunate position; the museum and art gallery had to be kept moderately warm if the valuable exhibits were to survive. There was a complicated system of three furnaces in our flat from which there were air ducts and pumps which would send the hot air up into the rooms upstairs. In the floors upstairs were large rectangular holes covered with ornate grids and here the warm air came out in a gentle stream but strong enough to lift females' skirts. If the museum was closed, it was most satisfactory on a cold day to stand above one of these grids but of course, the museum was not available for this purpose very often.

In the interests of fuel economy one of the furnaces was

shut down and another one had to be approached from the garden. These furnace rooms were not at all pleasant being covered in coal dust and stinking of coal fumes but if we were desperately cold we might spend a short while in one of them to, as it were, thaw out. The one indoor furnace room proved most useful in drying out the washing, as we were not allowed to hang out the washing in the garden, but it was somewhat difficult to ensure that the washing when dry was not dirtier than before its hand washing procedure – domestic washing machines had not been invented.

There was a separate large room for storing the coal, which had a gravitational chute into one of the furnace rooms, but as this coal room was always less than half-full, anxiously awaiting the next delivery of coal, much shovelling had to be done. The other furnace in use had an annexe for its supply of coal. These furnaces had to be attended to twice a day and normally one of the three attendants on my father's staff would carry out the very arduous task of riddling and filling the enormous furnaces.

During the war when manpower was severely limited, the attendants, in the winter evenings when the museum closed before dusk, could not be expected to return two hours later at 6 o'clock to feed these greedy monsters who demanded regular hours. In these circumstances, my father had to deal with the evening shift and the two shifts on Sundays. But we couldn't complain, because from the coal room we were able to take sufficient coal to light a fire in our drawing room (lounge) after lunch on cold days and there were many during the war years. We were lucky, the fact that we had one furnace in our flat roaring away meant that the extreme chill of a frosty day was somewhat diminished.

In addition, we had an electric fire that was just about portable and which we could switch on in the room we were using, if it happened to have a power point. Then there was the great difficulty in obtaining a new fire bar if it broke down. I can clearly remember some fire coils giving quite a miniature firework display before we were able to acquire a new one. However, this did not deter my sister, Paddy, and I crouching practically on top of the electric fire until our legs became all blotchy. My eldest sister, Ruth, would not deign to do this; she was of an age when the appearance of her legs was of greater importance to her; attractive stockings were seldom available!

In school, there was little heat except in the loos, which had radiators along one wall, and I am afraid some of us lingered longer than we should have particularly as the toilets were very modern and consequently quite pleasant rooms. I imagine the shops and stores were quite cold in winter but as we all had thick coats on, we didn't notice it except if we were trying on clothes and this did not occur often. No doubt, the shop assistants suffered from feeling the cold in the winter but everyone learnt 'to wrap up well'.

Public places of entertainment all seemed quite warm even on the coldest days but they were probably heated by body units. Cinemas, in particular, were mostly extremely well attended as an escape from the rigours of war but, strangely enough, the most successful films were those concerning war such as *Mrs Miniver* and *Gone with the Wind*. The Pavilion in Bournemouth continued to give a range of productions and I distinctly remember that if we arrived early we kept our coats on until the building filled up and the temperature rose. Needless to say there were times when attendances were poor; people, particularly at the beginning of the war, did not like going out in the blackout, but gradually they became accustomed to it and found that it was possible to see a little something in the dark when their eyes adjusted. There were times when air raids occurred and it seemed safer to stay at home in the Anderson or Morrison shelters.

The reason for all this suffering from the cold in winter

(chilblains were a norm) was that the country was almost completely reliant on coal for heating. There was no North Sea gas or nuclear energy. Both gas and electricity were obtained from the burning of coal. Then too, the demands of manufacturing soared as more and more planes, tanks, ships and armaments were required. It was not that there was a shortage of British coal; the problem was a shortage of labour. There was a Labour minister in the coalition government under Churchill whose name was Ernest Bevin and he realised that unless we produced more coal, the war effort would come to a grinding halt. Naturally, coal mining was a reserved occupation but many miners had volunteered to join the armed forces at the beginning of the war. Coal mining was not an enviable job; it was dark, dusty, unhealthy and dangerous. Bevin decided that conscripted men should be allocated to the mines and not always to the armed forces and the ones who served in the coal pits were known as the 'Bevin Boys'.

****

Many of the particular joys that we experienced before the war suffered. As we were growing up, and bedtime became later, my mother developed the habit of taking us out after our evening meal a couple of times a week for a special treat to the Ice Cream Parlour in the Square owned by Mr and Mrs Forte and here we would have our dessert or second course as we called it. It was a great treat to have a chocolate nut sundae or a fruit parfait or even a knickerbockers glory. For the first few weeks of the war this was feasible but soon there was the blackout to contend with. However, Mother was determined that this would not stop us. Shortly afterwards the Fortes were unable to obtain the ingredients they needed for the ice cream and a little later the Ice Cream Parlour suffered from extreme bomb damage and our ice cream treats ceased.

Mr Forte was the cousin of the London Fortes and the Bournemouth Fortes was quite independent of the large London concern. My mother became very friendly with Mrs Forte and she told us that Mr Forte's father lived in Boscombe and that every morning he cycled along the front at 5 o'clock in the morning to make the ice cream for the day in the small parlour wedged in between Bobbys (now Debenhams) and other shops. This branch of Fortes expanded in the Square and then in Westover Road to become well-known restaurants and Mrs Forte enjoyed arranging the décor in both restaurant complexes, a task in which she showed a great flair.

Another pre-war excitement which vanished from the calendar was Guy Fawkes Night – no bonfires and no fireworks. I must say that I was not altogether sorry about this because every party we had, there was always someone who let off 'bangers' right at me which terrified me but I did miss the beautiful Catherine wheels and the fun the next day collecting all the spent rockets.

Christmases suffered too. We celebrated them as best we could and Mummy always seemed to be lucky and obtained a turkey. We had a Christmas tree and some presents and I had my array of second hand books at the bottom of the bed. We played games: consequences, charades, hunt the thimble, table tennis and a game that caused great hilarity called wibbly wob. It was played rather like hockey with two teams alongside a long table and our sticks were composed of a firm handle with a long piece of most unstable wire on the end of which was fixed a small triangular pusher with which we had to shunt a small puck towards a goal.

For decorations round the house, we spent days making paper chains, which was fun and created a sense of anticipation for the important day that lay ahead. However, I did miss the visits to the big stores to Father Christmas' grottoes; these were either non-existent or extremely simple affairs, which made me aware of what I was missing. Then too, visits to toy departments were pretty miserable affairs – for at least a fortnight before Christmas the shelves were bare and even before this the variety of toys was extremely stinted. Woe betides anyone hoping to buy a present on Christmas Eve!

No, we had to follow more simple pursuits but surprisingly these sometimes were more enjoyable. We loved to skip, make up dances, walk on stilts or with books balanced on our heads and climb trees. We were never bored and we had never even heard of the word. Climbing trees was one of my particular pleasures and this came in extremely useful. We had quite an ancient mulberry tree in the garden which had grown in such a way that it was a delight to climb. When the mulberries developed, I was appointed mulberry picker and every day for probably three weeks, I scrambled up the tree and picked only the really black, luscious fruits; mulberries are almost inedible if picked with the slightest hint of red on them as at that stage they can be very sour. Left on the tree to ripen completely, there is hardly anything more delicious and I soon became quite an expert judge by dint of a little sampling, as was my wont in the presence of fruit berries.

The berries were not the only goodies that our mulberry tree had to offer; the leaves were a great contribution to the war effort and you may well wonder how. We collected them in great sacks and sent them down to a dear lady in North Dorset who kept silkworms. Mulberry leaves were the favourite food of silkworms and feasting on their favourite food, they showed their appreciation by spinning yards and yards of silk. In those days, parachutes were made of silk, which was strong and light at the same time. It was a comforting feeling that our little efforts probably saved the life of some poor airman so that he could fight again or maybe the life of our previously mentioned friend, Robert Stark, when he bailed out over Germany. It was a nice thought anyway!

77

The war sometimes presented fun games for us. One day we heard a plane flying overhead but there had been no siren to indicate that there were enemy planes about so we naturally assumed that it was one of ours. Presently we saw innumerable silver strips gently floating to the ground; what fun it was to collect as many of these as we possibly could and, needless to say we competed with each other to see who could collect the most. Naturally, we wondered what they were and later in the war when the secret of the British discovery of radar and its implementation was revealed, we suspected that a German aeroplane had been sent over to drop silver foil to discover if these strips would deflect the signals telling British forces where there were enemy planes. Presumably, the metal foil did not serve its purpose because we received no more presents of these metal strips.

Shrapnel from bombs was another collectors' item for children and even for some grown ups but we did not participate in this hobby – the ugly shapes of twisted and often razor sharp pieces of metal did not appeal to us, but many people decorated their mantelpieces with these awesome fragments.

****

It was amazing how fit war-children were overall, but maybe it wasn't so amazing because we were forced to eat simply and sensibly, and both poor and rich had good, wholesome food because of the rationing system. The price of food was kept low and shared out evenly; meat was actually rationed monetarily and if I remember rightly, it was one shilling and three pence a week, which is approximately 7p, so if one had a cheap cut of meat and made excellent stews the ration went further than having a leg of lamb. We used to have stew mid-week, a roast at the weekend, offal, which wasn't rationed but wasn't always available, on another day fish, which also wasn't rationed, when we could get it and vegetarian food on other days. All the meals were accompanied by lots of vegetables, which were cheap and fairly plentiful, and these were essential to fill up demanding tummies. Sugar, butter, and sweets either were rationed severely or were in short supply, i.e. under the counter. The government ruled that supplements were to be added to flour, in particular calcium, and the flour was no longer pure white and therefore bread contained some wheat germ and bran. Children received special allowances such as milk, cod liver oil, rose hip syrup and blackcurrant purée to ensure that they received enough vitamins and mineral salts.

We didn't suffer from lots of colds and flu; possibly because of posters and admonitions everywhere – 'Coughs and sneezes spread diseases, trap your germs in your handkerchiefs' or, as we said 'handkercheeses' to establish a rhyme that we could not forget.

This did not mean that we didn't have fears of illnesses but they were not the ones prevalent today. Science has eliminated some that we dreaded but new ones have evolved and others have become more common. Having read many Victorian and Edwardian novels, I was terrified of tuberculosis. Another ailment that I worried about was anaemia because several children we knew had died from this mysterious illness; it seemed that they were here today and gone the next, in spite of having to eat large amounts of raw liver – ugh!

Polio, we knew was either a crippler or a killer and there were epidemics of this horrible illness. Another germ I feared was pneumonia and I worried when I had a cold that it would suddenly turn into pneumonia. We were frequently admonished that if we got our feet wet or if we didn't wear enough clothes or we discarded our vests and liberty bodices we would catch pneumonia or have the death of a cold. Penicillin had been discovered but was not in general use until after the war.

The main killers of nowadays, heart disease and cancer did not unduly worry us; these diseases, in our thoughts, were reserved for those people who had passed the allotted span of three score years and ten. Aids, Legionnaire's Disease and bird flu did not exist.

As for the childhood illnesses of measles, German measles, mumps, whooping cough, and chickenpox, we thought that they were unpleasant matters that we probably had to endure but at the same time, they were good for a few weeks off school since, at that time long quarantine conditions were strictly enforced. I recall one small school being closed completely because one of the boarders had suspected mumps. In consequence of these restrictions, many children grew up without suffering from these illnesses only to catch them when they were adult and when these diseases were much more serious.

****

Youngsters growing up during the war were just as much interested in 'pop' music as 'teenagers' are today although neither of those words had been invented then. The music usually came from catchy tunes and songs in films – there were no pop groups writing their own songs or using material supplied to them, but nevertheless the interest was probably as great. We had wind up gramophones and our parents had a posh radiogram on which my father played his classical music. The records were made of shellac and were easily broken. Each side lasted no more than three minutes which was all right for our 'pop' records but a symphony required innumerable discs and every few minutes the record had to be changed. Some very expensive radiograms had mechanical means to play a number of records one after another, the classical albums being arranged so that this could be done. The steel needles used to play records had to be changed every now and then when they became blunt and if a mellow sound without too much scratchy noise was required, special needles could be purchased. I believe that these latter ones were made of hawthorn (that's what our father told us) and had to be replaced frequently as they were quickly blunted with use. And what did we listen to?

At the beginning of the war, Gracie Fields was singing. As a young girl, she worked in a cotton factory where the noise of the machines was almost deafening and she loved to sing, so naturally she developed an extremely strong voice that the British public loved to hear and so she became 'Our Gracie'. Following her was Vera Lynn, who quickly became the 'Forces Favourite'. She was young and beautiful, had a charming voice and could be heard on *Forces Favourites*, a radio programme of requests devised for the services abroad. Like many of the entertainers of the war era, she often travelled overseas to cheer up our soldiers fighting in foreign fields; all this was organised by ENSA. Many of the songs that Vera Lynn sung are still heard and enjoyed today. They were usually romantic and were about situations that mainly occur in wartime; for example *Wish Me Luck As You Wave Me Goodbye*, *The White Cliffs Of Dover*, *We'll Meet Again*, *I'll Be With You In Apple Blossom Time* and *Don't Sit Under The Apple Tree With Anyone Else But Me*. Strangely enough a most popular song that everyone sung originated in Germany and was translated into English. It was *Lili Marlene* and was associated with army barracks.

Across the 'Pond', two American rivals fought it out; Frank Sinatra and Bing Crosby were the popular singers of the day. Frank Sinatra made the young girls swoon, a phenomenon new to us, and which I failed to understand. Bing Crosby crooned away beautifully to us, and he was my choice of the two, but the music most connected with the war came from the baton of Glenn Miller. He conducted a 'Big Band' with the American

Glenn Miller

Frank Sinatra

82

The Andrews Sisters

Bing Crosby

83

air force and probably did more than any one else to popularise the 'Big Band' sound.

Glenn Miller and his band did much to raise the morale of the armed forces but unfortunately, he went missing on an aeroplane flight, much to the dismay of thousands of fans. It was never discovered what happened to the plane he was travelling on.

Another bandleader who was very popular in Britain was Victor Silvester. His music was strictly dance tempo and was appreciated by all ballroom dancers. He was really not into jitterbugging and jive, which became extremely popular when the American forces arrived in England. I am afraid that I, with most of my friends, was not daring enough to jitterbug (all that upside down stuff and swirling around showed off too much underwear if only in brief flashes) but we did like the more sedate jiving.

Across the Atlantic, the Andrew Sisters were raising the morale of the Americans and they too travelled the world entertaining the forces with such songs as *Boogie Woogie Bugle Boy*, *Don't Fence Me In* and *Money Is The Root Of All Evil*. These girls were probably the nearest thing to a modern pop group.

There was also popular music such as *The Warsaw Concerto* inspired by war events. In complete contrast, there were some zany numbers which were accompanied by special dances such as *The Lambeth Walk*, *Underneath the Spreading Chestnut Tree* and the *Hokey Cokey*.

In the early part of the war, many of the jolliest songs of the 30s lingered on and I recall a news item that described the rescue of some sailors who had been torpedoed and had spent a horrific week in an open boat in the middle of the Atlantic. These men kept their spirits up by singing *Roll Out The Barrel*. The first thing that they asked for after they were rescued was a cigarette.

At that time, cigarettes were considered ideal for raising the spirits of our brave servicemen! The harmful results that tobacco has on health had not been discovered then; anyway, its beneficial effects on nerves was important at such critical moments.

****

The reader may be interested in wartime fashions which were much influenced by the conditions of the time. First, we have to begin with the fashionable shape; women were expected to be curvaceous and definitely not skinny. I, unfortunately, was most undesirably thin and friends, grown ups in particular, would greet me with, "Are you all right, Joy?" My immediate response would have been to say, "Why" but I was too shy. I soon learnt what was coming next, "But you are so thin, are you sure you are well?" Even my best friend used to tease me about my bony appearance.

We had a delightfully young teacher (very rare because most graduates had joined the forces) and we enjoyed her history lessons but when she was asked to teach us Current Affairs in the sixth form, which we were hoping would be about the latest news concerning the war, we were so disappointed when she began dictating to us notes about the 1920s, that my friend and I made every effort to be sent out. It was really quite simple, we began whispering to each other rather loudly until presently our teacher sent us out of the room. This was a practice that worked with several teachers; once we were sent out, we quickly made our way to the library that we both loved so much. Not only was it in three most delightfully sunny rooms but also it contained many books and magazines including *National Geographic* magazines.

On one of these occasions, my friend pointed out to me an article about starving people often engendered by war conditions and there was one most appealing picture of a starving baby. She assured me that it had a strong resemblance to me and it was entitled 'undernourished baby' which she abbreviated to 'Unby', and this became my nickname until the end of that term. Fortunately, this word was forgotten over the holidays and my usual nickname 'Joybells' thankfully returned.

Typical wartime fashion as worn by my sisters

So the fashion dictated no appearance of bones and particularly no knobbly knees. However, there were certain parts of the body which should not be accentuated, one of them was the bottom and so a straight back view was desirable. In line with a martial look, shoulders had to be pronounced and this was achieved by adding most generous shoulder pads in garments and this appearance was sometimes emphasised by the addition of epaulets. The clothes we wore, all pandered to this currently desirable shape.

However, there were the constrictions of wartime to be incorporated into the clothes we wore. The main influence was the shortage of material, which meant that all women's clothing stopped abruptly at the middle of the knee and was tight fitting. There were few pleats and certainly no swirlingly flared skirts; blouses and shirts were cut with the minimum of material. Dresses hugged the body and waists were accentuated, although for a short time, dropped waistlines were fashionable.

Another consideration was keeping warm, particularly in the winter, and so coats and costumes were popular. As I grew up, I wore a costume under my coat when going out in the winter. This concern about keeping warm led to what was known as a siren suit; the modern equivalent might be a boiler suit in an extremely warm woolly material. But the siren suit had something extra, namely a buttoned flap at the back, which simplified visits to the toilet. So many of the wartime fashions were practical and this particular outfit fitted the lifestyle of people in heavily blitzed towns who had to rush to the air raid shelters at night, particularly to the inhabitants of London who lived in the tubes at night and surfaced during the day to try to go about their usual business if their work place or home had not been reduced to a pile of rubble during the night.

Normally, women wore skirts (less material) even in the armed forces. However, there were certain jobs where trousers were more suitable and this applied to some factory work, but these trousers were not fashion items and jeans had not yet been introduced to this country.

Fashion changed little during the war years because clothes were rationed by means of clothes coupons and we wore our clothes almost until they disintegrated or, in my case, grew out of them, at which time I inherited my sisters' discarded clothes. One of my sisters, who was very clothes conscious, would alter garments that she no longer liked, or take them up to a dressmaker if it was a more dramatic change that she wanted.

On the whole, wartime dress was rather drab; colourful dyes were in short supply and some even unattainable because they came from Germany. One of these colours was turquoise and I believe bright emerald green was difficult to obtain and I was particularly bucked when my mother bought me a costume in dazzling green.

Stockings were another problem – heavy lisle stockings were obtainable but silk ones rarely appeared in the shops and these were what young girls wanted to wear. Of course, there was a black market in rare items and people occasionally paid the extortionate prices that the spivs charged but this was considered most unpatriotic and was rarely undertaken. Mostly young ladies sported bare legs and only resorted to the heavy duty stockings in cold weather, but they were not averse to beautifying their legs with a beige or light brown make-up and applying a darker line down the back to simulate the seam that all stockings had at that time and if there was not time for the full works, then just a seam was applied in a brownish colour. There were no nylon stockings until towards the end of the war when American soldiers brought them over as presents for English girls that they might meet.

Shoe shops offered a very narrow selection and customers had to be satisfied with what was available in their size. Shoes were made of leather and the soles wore out quickly so the cobbler was much in demand. Some pre-war soles, particularly those of sandals, were made of crepe rubber and this was a more hardwearing substance, but rubber had to be imported and was much needed for the war effort. Plastics and composition rubber did not exist although the Germans, I believe, managed to produce some ersatz rubber. The enemy fortunately did not have tropical colonies which could supply genuine rubber and this must have hampered their fighting power.

Like clothes fashions, hairstyles changed little during the war. Coiffures, if you can call them that, had to be practical and that meant, on the whole, being short or done in such a way that it seemed short. Girls in the forces were not allowed to have hair dangling below their collars and long hair was not allowed in factories in case it became caught up in the machinery. In fact, in many factories and in places where food was being dealt with, hair had to be tied up with a scarf or a cap had to be worn. Even in school, we were not allowed to have hair that touched our collars. Having a rather short neck, I was frequently told that I must tie my hair back. The trouble occurred because, in common with many girls who had straight hair, I used to have a 'perm' (curly or wavy hair was the preferred style) and my mother did not like us having these rather primitive curling devices more than once a year because she thought that they were damaging to the hair. Consequently, towards the end of the year, my hair was becoming quite long, but not really long enough to tie back without it looking silly and if I cut my hair, I lost my curls. After serious threats from my form mistress, I decided to practise a rather naughty joke on my teacher. I set the alarm very early one morning and spent a long time pinning up my hair in a most elaborate style known as Edwardian which was worn only by the most sophisticated ladies for special functions. I thought my form mistress would be horrified but would not be able to admonish me because my hair was no longer touching my collar. What a brilliant teacher she was! I met her in the corridor and she greeted me with, "How attractive your hair looks, Joy!" The laugh was on me as the saying goes. Needless to say, I didn't get up early the next morning to arrange my hair; I just hoicked it back with an elastic band and envied my class mates who all seemed to have lovely long necks.

Curls were very much the 'in thing' and most people who had straight hair spent much time putting curlers in their hair.

Many women, every night before they went to bed, wound there hair round anything from pipe cleaners (comfortable) to small cylinders of rubber or Bakelite and my sisters were no exception. Of course, the curl did not last long, especially if the weather was wet and some women took to keeping the curlers in all day and covering their hair with a scarf in a turban like knot and releasing their hair for a night out ballroom dancing or visiting the pub with their boy friend or husband. Some older women rarely seemed to take their hair out of the curlers and a number could not even be bothered to cover up their hair curlers – probably they were waiting for their husbands to come back from the war.

One of the great entertainments of the war was the cinema and young girls liked to copy the looks of the various film stars and there was one famous star, Veronica Lake, who had long straight blonde hair which she wore sexily covering up one eye and for a short while girls emulated this look, not that the word 'sex' was ever used in polite company. Of course, this style was not at all practical during a war situation and so it didn't catch on.

Make up; most women wore some form of make up and by coincidence, it wasn't far away for Bournemouth girls. The famous Max Factor company had a factory at Wallisdown, and this American firm coined the phrase 'The make up of the Stars' and marketed what was called pancake make up. This was a very heavy sort of powder and many of us did not like it because it looked most artificial. On the other hand it hid blemishes and wrinkles.

Most of us preferred a more natural look assisted by a light make up. Rouge or what one might call nowadays blusher was available and worn if needed. Lipstick was extremely popular and was applied thickly in bright colours. Strangely enough, our dentist ran a sideline in kiss-proof lipsticks; these were strange because the lipstick was a bright orange in its holder but when applied changed colour and this colour varied with each person. It seemed like magic to us and it was actually made by our dentist in his laboratory. I don't think it was absolutely kiss-proof, but it did not leave a mark on a cup or glass which was something. Eye make up was not in fashion and the few girls who wore it were considered rather flighty if not worse.

Fashion for men was almost non-existent; the style that men were wearing prior to the war continued to be worn throughout the war. Men who might have had an influence on fashion were in uniform and didn't need to buy clothes until they were demobbed and then they were presented with a choice of demob suits. A few of what we called 'spivs' chose to wear somewhat flashy suits but on the whole civilian clothes were pretty drab. My father was the exception; before the war, he had discovered attractive Swiss velour sweaters and began to make a collection of them. At that time, he chose artistic colours but when the war broke out the supplies ceased.

However, it was not long before my father discovered that he could buy second hand ones at the Red Cross shops and by this time he had caught the collector's bug and he would purchase them in any colour that was going – many of them were women's sweaters and so were to be found in extremely colourful shades. He bought them regardless and of course he wore them, parading through the staid streets of Bournemouth such as Westover Road, Old Christchurch Road and Commercial Road. I remember one day when we were accompanying my parents, my sister, Paddy, said, "Let's drop behind and pretend we don't belong."

Father also resorted to dyeing a rather tired looking shantung suit a delicate shade of salmon. Needless-to-say, he received many strange stares because this was certainly unusual in the war years. In men's clothing, there was again the economy of material and double-breasted suits became single-breasted and turn-ups on trousers were discontinued. The reader may not consider this a fashion point but our brave pilots and aircrew adopted a craze of having dirty caps. At first it was genuinely earned dirt such as oil, smoke and even blood stains but later, some of the new arrivals on action duty deliberately simulated such stains using beer, red wine and grease. What was certain, was that all of these airmen hung onto their battered caps with great tenacity.

Retribution

It was in the Summer of 1941 that the first sign of hope lit the war scene although, at the time, the British general public was not aware of its great significance. This was the time that Hitler made his first enormous error; he did not appreciate that the same error had been committed before by Napoleon, or maybe he thought that his modern armed forces were invincible. Anyway, he decided to invade Russia in June, which in his estimation was early enough to capture Moscow and bring Russia to its knees prior to Christmas and before the arctic conditions of this part of the world really set in. Germany deliberately ignored its non-aggression pact with Russia; dare one say it in view of the terrible suffering that the Russian people endured, but maybe the Russians deserved such treachery since they had broken a similar pact that was proposed with Britain and France in 1939 in order to share with Germany the spoils of Poland.

Maybe history will tell us that there might not have been a war if Russia had adhered to its prior agreement with Britain and France. The excellent propaganda of 1941 convinced us that our new allies were great friends of Britain and that Stalin was an exemplary leader of his people. The British public knew nothing of the atrocities that the Dictator of Russia had committed; the invasions of Poland and Finland were pushed out of our minds and we began to admire the Russian people and their leaders. For the first time for many months, we were not alone in defending the world against the axis powers.

An even greater hope of ultimate victory came later in the year when the Japanese attacked the United States navy in Pearl Harbour. This brought the might of the U.S.A. to our aid; previously they had helped our efforts by supplying us with arms under a Lease Lend agreement but after 1941, their enormous wealth and strength was set to winning a war against evil aggression.

Maybe, the Americans with their industrial and military power did win the war as they like to think, but it could not have been won at all without Britain and her Empire holding the fort, as it were, during those dark years of 1939 – 1941.

Coming to more personal matters on the Home Front and how it affected our lives, naturally we followed the course of events, which was now on a global scale. The atlas was well thumbed. I discovered where the sieges of Leningrad (now St Petersburg as it had been prior to the Revolution) and Stalingrad were, and I eventually found Velikiye Luki on the map. It seemed that the fighting round this town went on for months and I heard this name on the wireless day after day. I interpreted it as Leeky Lukey. The brave Russian stand in this area probably prevented the Germans from taking Moscow.

Then the great retreat of the Germans came, as they were not equipped to fight in the harsh conditions of a Russian winter. We were told that many Germans froze to death as their clothing was inadequate and their lines of communication were so vast that fresh supplies could not get through. As for the war in the Far East, there was even more thumbing of the Atlas; I followed the general outline of the fighting but so many of the Pacific Islands had strange names that I found it difficult to remember them even then and I certainly cannot recall them today.

****

The whole effect of the German's concentration on Russia was a slight respite from the intensive bombing that Britain had been receiving. Then with the welcoming of thousands and thousands of army and air force reinforcements from overseas, the situation was changing from one of defence to that of

94

offence and the ultimate aim of the Allies in our sector of the war was the invasion of Europe. The forces had to be gathered and trained in Britain and as 'D.Day' (Deliverance Day, June 6th 1944) approached, all the army forces involved descended on the South coast. In preparation for this invasion, the intensive bombing of Germany was imperative and so countless airmen arrived in relays in Bournemouth where they stayed for a few weeks awaiting posting to an airfield. Most of them came from Canada, which had developed special training camps for airmen, but that did not mean to say they were all Canadian. There were many other Dominion countries represented and even British airmen who were frequently sent over to Canada for training.

The air force commandeered all the large empty hotels which surrounded us to house these men. The first impact that this had on our lives was that my parents didn't think it suitable for three young girls to sleep out of doors in a sheltered alcove on camp beds, particularly as two of us were nearly grown up. The Royal Bath Hotel was right next door and there was an access gate between the gardens of the museum and the hotel. This alteration to our lives did not particularly perturb us and my sisters initially found fun in directing binoculars into the windows of the hotel to find out what was going on next door. Strangely enough, we learnt from some of the airmen whom we met in our shared garden that they, too, were training binoculars on our windows!

As the German raids on this country diminished a little, the air personnel required was for bomber aircraft to take the war into the enemy's territory and so the men billeted in these former luxury hotels were very varied. Of course there were pilots, but they were outnumbered by navigators, bombers, wireless operators and gunners, each identifiable with the badges on their uniforms. Arguably, the tail gunner was the most vulnerable as he was the enemy fighter pilot's first target.

As to their destinations and time of departure from Bournemouth, it was a closely guarded secret and we played a little joke on some of these airmen, which took them by surprise telling them that their destination was the Far East and that they would be leaving within the week. How did we know? If this was to be their destination in the near future, then their faces would turn yellow, and not, I would hastily add, to match the Japanese, but to prevent them from catching malaria. The injection ministered produced this unpleasant effect. Aircrew who returned to Bournemouth after their tour of operations awaited a transfer to a British airfield so we were fortunate enough to renew some acquaintances.

We met many of these charming men and life became a roller coaster – the joy of welcoming these young men and then the sadness of their departure knowing full well the terrors that they would inevitably meet and that many would never return to their families and loved ones. Naturally there were some we became very attached to and then it was extremely miserable to have to say, "Farewell." Sometimes we kept in touch by letter but this was quite difficult and there was intense censorship, so it was hard even to read between the lines.

****

How did we meet all these young airmen? Well, it was hard not to, as we were surrounded by them and it seemed our duty to welcome them to our shores. But in the main, we worked in canteens and charities that offered entertainment and light refreshments in an attempt to cheer up the strangers to our shores. There was one particular charity, the Knights of St Columbus which took over the beach café to the east of Bournemouth pier and had a canteen there (more of that later) but perhaps one of the favourite haunts of the officers was Lady Ryder's establishment at the White Hermitage, a former

96

hotel opposite the pier.

Perhaps I should not have used the word 'establishment'; it might provoke undesirable translations in the reader's mind. I can assure you that it was a most worthy organisation – the strongest drink that was served was tea and all the volunteers who worked there had to be introduced by someone who was already helping. There was a lounge where tea was served at 4 o'clock in a typically English style, a small ballroom and an annexe where table tennis could be played. In fact it most resembled a tea dance every afternoon and at 6 o'clock, it was closed. My eldest sister was soon invited to help by one of the volunteers and because it was somewhat out of her experience, she took along my other sister for company and support.

They enjoyed working at the White Hermitage and attended twice a week regularly for some time, but then my eldest sister finished her course at College and was called up to manage a canteen away from the Bournemouth area.

My sister, Paddy, had cold feet about going to the White Hermitage alone and so she pleaded with me to accompany her. At first I refused on the grounds that I was much too young; my sisters were virtually grown up, but I was still a child and a very small one at that and in addition incredibly shy. However, Paddy was most persuasive telling me that all I had to do was hand round cups of tea, sandwiches and cakes and play a little table tennis if I wanted. It all sounded so simple and not exactly terrifying so I eventually consented. The reader may note that no mention was made of a ballroom and dancing. Well, we arrived, passing it seemed, innumerable airmen who whistled at my sister because she was very glamorous and obviously she knew some of them who greeted her warmly.

I found myself alone and petrified and someone placed a cup of tea into my hand, which I offered to the nearest airman who promptly asked me to dance with him. I was too shy to say

97

that I hadn't learnt to dance and anyway, I thought that perhaps the art of dancing was one of the attributes that the 'handers out' of tea were supposed to have. My ballroom dancing experience was practically nil.

Just before the war, my mother had insisted that her young daughters should learn to dance, "It is part of a young girl's education." My father was very much a puritan and considered dancing evil and so quite a feud broke out. Eventually my mother took the matter into her own hands and knowing nothing about the different types of dancing arranged for her three daughters to have a lesson every Friday evening for an hour. She decided that we should do a quarter of an hour of tap dancing, a further quarter of an hour ballroom dancing and then half an hour of ballet, all this at the Norman and Saxon School of Dancing, which was above Burtons the outfitters of gentlemen's clothing, in the Square.

I am surprised that the dancing school agreed to it because it involved bringing in three teachers but in those days, the customer was always right. After about four lessons, we gave up the ballroom dancing but continued the tap dancing because we liked it and we had seen Shirley Temple tapping away expertly and, of course, as children we adored her. We continued with ballet, carrying on into the early part of the war until bombs exploding in the Square somewhat damaged the dancing school.

So, I had had approximately one-hour's ballroom tuition when I was ushered on to the ballroom floor with knees like jelly out of sheer fright. At the same time, I was attempting to put on the air of an experienced dancer.

That first day at Lady Ryder's I didn't hand round a single sandwich or play any table tennis, I danced for two hours and I was almost beginning to enjoy it! Thereafter I accompanied my sister each time she went, usually wearing some of her clothes and trying, although small, to look somewhat grown up.

Naturally, we soon became acquainted with many airmen and once more my mother came up trumps. She encouraged us to invite these young men home and I think they enjoyed being in a family atmosphere – they were so young, most of them not much more than 19.

We often invited them to meals when rations allowed and we discovered that one thing they all missed was a glass of milk. I hated milk and, of course, I had a child's allowance of milk so there was plenty to go around.

The most popular entertainment at home was table tennis and many of them liked exploring the museum in the evening when it was shut. Some of them liked to go for walks and so we could show them our beautiful town of Bournemouth. Some of them liked to take us to the pictures, but they always had to ask my father first since he considered the cinema 'the house of Beelzebub' and he needed to know what the film was about. I used to think how can anyone know if they haven't seen it?

The newspapers of those days did not seem to have Entertainment Pages giving critiques of the latest films and anyway these airmen probably did not read the local papers. However, Father never refused to let us go, so presumably he was satisfied with their replies.

Christmas was a special time to make sure that these brave young men who had come to fight for us in our hour of need did not feel too desperately home sick, so everyone made a big effort to ensure that no airman who wanted to be with a family over the holiday period was disappointed. Lady Ryder's organisation had offers of hospitality from all over the country and many of the young men travelled to families far away but also many stayed in the Bournemouth area to spend the Christmas Days with local families.

We usually managed to save up enough rations to invite three or four for Christmas Day and it was a very jolly party of about 12 that gathered round the large oval table in the

Museum. We played many crazy party games and, of course, table tennis and the ever-popular wibbly wob, which the Canadians readily took to because we played it with ice hockey rules, their national sport.

****

I mentioned earlier the Knights of St Columbus and their canteen at Bournemouth pier. One of my school pals was asked to help at this evening venue for the airmen and again I was asked along to, as it were, give support; it was always quite nerve racking to go to these ventures on one's own. I was a little older this time and did not feel so conscious of being still a child amongst grown ups, all of whom were men. Our duties were to serve up food and drinks (non-alcoholic), take the money, clear the tables and wash up. We just mixed in and did the different jobs as and when they were needed, quite amicably so no one was stuck at any one task for any length of time. We thoroughly enjoyed the work and we were able to pass the time of day with many young airmen but we were extremely busy, so conversation was very limited.

When the canteen closed at 10 p.m., we had to clear up and then we lined up to receive our pay, a choice of one of the following: a tin of fruit, a delicious fruit pie, packet of cookies or a large bar of chocolate. I always chose a tin of peaches, something to take home; the others I would have probably eaten before I reached the doorstep and my choice was always rewarded by the general appreciation of the family.

Getting home was the problem because we didn't leave the canteen before 11 p.m. and this was not the time of day for young girls to be walking alone in the blackout.

My friend lived on the west cliff and I lived on the east cliff, not far away from each other as the crow flies and in fact one of our pastimes was to go on to our respective roofs at an appointed time and wave large hankies to each other. I don't think our watches were well synchronised or perhaps we were looking at the wrong roofs, because we never saw one another's hankies; maybe they were too small!

Usually my friend escorted me to my house because it was nearer but if we thought that we heard or glimpsed something suspicious, I would accompany my friend up the west cliff to her home. Again if there seemed to be something a little strange on the way back, we would go to my house and this procedure would sometimes go on for quite a long time until our fears were allayed; nevertheless the last trip was always extremely fraught. It was worse on windy nights when leaves or bits of litter were blowing about. It is amazing how, when you can't see anything, the imagination takes over and turns a leaf blowing in the wind into footfalls sneaking up behind you.

****

Shortly after beginning work at the canteen, I was asked by the American army officers club at the Marsham Court Hotel, just across the road from the Museum, to hostess there once or twice a week. I suppose by this time I was becoming more used to dealing with a crowd of young men and so I boldly tackled the task on my own, without a hand to hold, but this was somewhat different. I did not expect to meet a crowd of high-ranking officers, most of them nearly old enough to be my grandfather. Needless to say, I was mightily overawed and then I spotted one young face wending his way towards me. He was not an officer and probably felt like a fish out of water, as I did. He happened to be a keen photographer and his senior officer had asked for a volunteer to be his publicity photographer. So he was nicknamed the 'Colonel' and he followed his commanding officer everywhere in case the opportunity arose for a photo shot, which could be sent back to the U.S.A. to the commanding officer's local newspaper.

The 'Colonel', Charles Hulse, in the darkroom

This officer was really genned up on publicity. I think we both held each other's hands, not literally, amongst these high-ranking officers (my new found friend was just 19). Visits to this club were hard because small talk proved difficult and most other subjects could not be entered into because of security reasons as these were the gentlemen staying briefly in Bournemouth who were planning and organising the 'D.Day' invasion of Europe. Few of them were interested in dancing. Rumours went around that Eisenhower and Montgomery and possibly even Churchill met at the Carlton Hotel on the east cliff for vital planning decisions regarding the imminent invasion, but all was 'hush hush'.

On one of these visits to Marsham Court, I heard the good news that a coach outing was to be organised and I was invited.

102

It was to be to Highcliffe Castle and the historic town of Christchurch. Locals knew virtually nothing about a castle in the village of Highcliffe because it was privately owned and was not open to the public but the family had honoured the U.S.A. Army Officers' Club with an invitation to look over the 19th century castle.

When I climbed on the coach, I was faced with a sea of army officers' faces and not a single female was present. I was expecting to see several of the lady volunteers there. However, there was, fortunately, 'The Colonel' who had kept a seat for me. It had occurred to his commanding officer that it seemed likely on this expedition there would be a suitable photo shot that he could send back to his local paper in the U.S.A.

Arriving at Highcliffe Castle, we were warmly welcomed by Mrs Stuart Wortley to her home. I do not recall any more of her presence, because I was so overawed by the magnificence of the grand hall with its twin staircase and potted palms. My imagination ran riot peopling the stairs with Hollywood stars gracefully descending to a most glittering ball. Its size and luxuriance as an entrance hall impressed me so much that I didn't take in much more of the building apart from the library which amazed me by seemingly holding as many books as a public library. Of course to put these impressions in perspective, I must point out that I had never previously visited a stately home. In the mid 20th century, such residences open to the public were quite rare and during the war many of these huge homes were commandeered to accommodate service personnel. I remember being slightly disappointed that we were not led out into the extensive garden and grounds, but maybe the coastal defences or a shortage of time prohibited such an excursion. These officers had much important work to do and this charming expedition was, as it was for me, a break from the rigours of war.

Modern day Highcliffe Castle

After the visit to the castle, we were whisked away in the coach to Christchurch where a restaurant near the Priory served up an English cream tea. I guess that some of the food supplies for this sumptuous repast had been provided by the U.S.A. army. This restaurant had a garden that backed immediately onto the ruins of the ancient Norman castle and the antiquity of these remains fascinated the Americans. They could not believe that they were looking at something almost 900 years old and I was able to answer a few of their questions somewhat sketchily from my schoolgirl knowledge of history. I had never actually seen these ruins before but I was aware of their existence. Needless to say, I was more interested in the delights of the tea table; what an escape from the rigours of rationing.

The Americans did not consume their tea with the enthusiasm that I experienced but then there was no shortage of food for these officers. The American army in England experienced plentiful supplies of food and the officers, in particular, fed off the fat of the land. I have included an authentic day's menu of the choices offered to army officers, but I gather the ordinary G.I. sometimes resented the luxury diet that their officers enjoyed. I would probably have been delighted to share in the G.I.'s food but I certainly did not resent their abundance of food, because they had come to our aid when we were in need of help and they were probably incredibly homesick. Also, they were soon to be part of the greatest invasion of all time.

****

'The Colonel', real name Charles Hulse, had quite a short stay in Bournemouth before his unit was posted to Europe, but we got to know him well, because my mother, as was her wont, invited him round and he took to visiting us most days generously bringing us boxes of chocolate and other goodies.

Luckily, he missed the Normandy landings when the Americans were slaughtered in vast numbers on Omaha Beach and his unit entered the battlefield when the allied armies had advanced far into France and Belgium but he did get involved in the ferocious Battle of the Bulge when the Germans made an unexpected fierce counter attack. It seems strange, but he had no idea that the British were fighting in this invasion of Europe. They were aware that they were fighting side by side with Canadians but no news was given them of the British army.

I knew little of this at the time in spite of correspondence with Charles Hulse whilst this was happening. Naturally, strict censorship prevented any war news being mentioned in letters, so all his correspondence was cheerful and full of jokes, even one letter being written round and round the paper finishing up

105

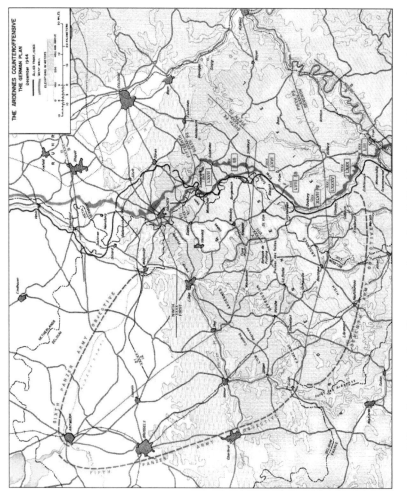

Map showing the German plans for 'The Battle of the Bulge'

Charles Hulse, 'The Colonel', taking prisoners

Charles Hulse with flag taken at captured Mauser house

107

in the centre. I found it incredibly difficult to answer his letters so my side of the correspondence was rather dilatory. What could I write about? Our lives were wonderful compared with what the invasion forces were enduring, so it seemed to me unfair to write about my activities and there was no shared background or any length of friendship and, as he was just a friend, all romantic words were out of the question. What could I say to cheer him up?

I learnt, many, many moons later, that he had resumed his official work as wireless operator, because his commander no longer required his services as photographer since there were official war photographers at work. I also learnt that single handed, he captured three German soldiers and being the first person to enter the Mauser's house, he liberated the German flag.

The firm of Mauser produced most of the rifles used by the Germans during the war and the factory and the Mauser home were situated on the east side of the River Rhine, over which our friend Charles Hulse and the 78th Infantry Division crossed on the only bridge that the Germans had failed to blow up.

Then many years later (approximately 55), thanks to the worldwide Internet, the 'Colonel' contacted me through the Russell Cotes Museum and informed me of his exploits during the invasion of Germany. Charles also confessed that he had pinched one of our table tennis balls. While we were clearing up after a game of table tennis, he found a ball lying on the floor and in his joking mind, he thought, next time that I play table tennis, I will say that I have brought my own ball and so he drew the well-known character of Kilroy with the words 'Kilroy was here'. The British called this cartoon figure 'Mr. Chad'. Unfortunately, the time for the joke never came because he was posted to Europe the very next day. However, he thought that the table tennis ball brought him luck and ensured his survival and when he eventually returned to America, he

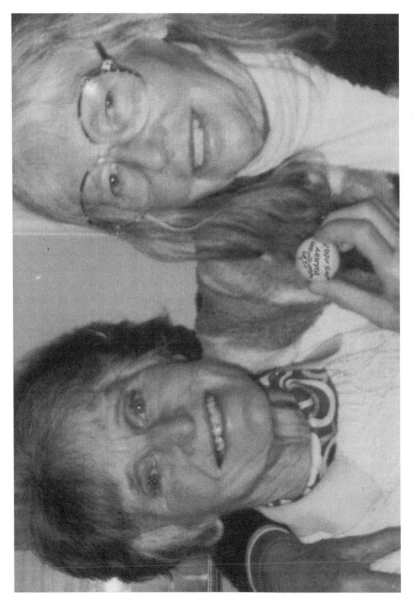

Joy Shellard and her sister Paddy with the table tennis ball

carefully stowed it in a drawer.

After contacting me in 2000, he remembered his carefully preserved souvenir of Bournemouth and when I visited my sister in the U.S.A. he sent it to us. The story of this ball intrigued local newspapers both sides of the Atlantic. Bournemouth Echo's Ed Perkins contacted Charles Hulse for his side of the story and constructed a most amusing article which then crossed the Atlantic to appear in newspaper articles over in the U.S. A.

I must apologise for jumping around in time, but because of censorship, I did not know anything about the Colonel's exploits during the war at the time.

****

Meanwhile in Bournemouth, there was much fun to be had, but perhaps we could console our consciences that we were maybe helping some of the soldiers and airmen to temporarily forget the horrors of war and what they were about to face in the near future.

It was ironical that the ice rink that had been forced to close immediately the war began because it had a glass roof, was converted by the Canadian air force into a beautiful ballroom with a maple floor and dances were held there two or three times a week. Certain nights were officers' evenings and on others it was reserved for 'the ranks'. To these dances, airmen invited young girls they knew and my sisters and I really enjoyed going to the former ice rink because there was plenty of space and the sprung floor was a delight on which to dance. The bands that played were Big Bands composed of airmen and the music was very Glenn Miller in style. There was plenty of space for jiving and jitterbugging, but we also had conventional waltzes, foxtrots and quicksteps.

Half way through the evening, there were refreshments which were very agreeable to ration starved Bournemouth girls but no alcohol was served so there was no hanging round the bar by the men. Later on there was a 'jam' session when it seemed that all dancing stopped. The Canadians gathered round the soloist who was usually a drummer and clapped and cheered. I am afraid that this didn't particularly attract me – I wanted to dance and my tapping feet could hardly refrain from moving about.

****

Something else my friend and I enjoyed doing was cycling out to Longham, just north of Bournemouth, where there was a riding school. The land round about was mainly open heath land and so was absolutely ideal for horse riding. It may seem strange to the reader that, in this mechanised era, horses were still, in the middle of the 20th century, required for the war effort and because of this riding schools could only acquire the halt, the lame, the blind and the ancient, so we had strange but fairly docile nags to ride. My friend was usually allotted the horse that was blind in one eye, which was difficult to restrain from veering into hedges that were frequently composed of holly or gorse. I usually struggled with a lame one; I clearly remember my first experience on one of these horses. I think that it must have been an old one, nice and slow but solely interested in returning to her stall for food.

Outside the stables was the main road to Bournemouth, which was usually quiet during the war due to petrol restrictions. At this point there was a fork with a pointed piece of land in between the main road and the lesser road. All the horses crossed safely on to the narrow land between the two roads and then safely across the minor road, all except mine who just refused to follow. I abhorred the thought of kicking her and no encouragement would pressurise this elderly lady horse into going forward. If I released her reins, she immediately turned to go back to the stables but I wanted to join the others on a countryside trot. Then, to my surprise, the main road suddenly filled with a convoy of army vehicles. There was mile upon mile of tanks, lorries, jeeps, motor cycles and large gun carriers. It seemed as if a whole army was being moved! In fact that wasn't far from the truth because this was just before D.Day and the invasion of Europe.

There I was stuck, the horse wouldn't go forward and we couldn't go back. I think I was there, very scared, for a quarter of an hour. These armoured vehicles seemed to consume the road and even encroached on my tiny piece of land. What if this horse, a stranger to me, took fright and bolted? If I dismounted and she went wild, I would be in a precarious position. However, she was just about controllable if I could stop her from turning round and trotting back to her stall through the massive convoy that was driving almost bumper to bumper.

Then, suddenly there was silence and the peace of the countryside was restored. A kindly gentleman having seen my predicament sauntered up to me and explained the workings of a horse's mind. He suggested that if I released my firm hold on the horse's reigns, she would go. I explained that the horse would go the opposite way to where I wanted to go, but he wasn't listening and by that time I knew that the riding party would be far ahead and I would get lost looking for them, so I followed the gentleman's instructions and the horse and I quickly turned round and trotted back to the stables where, I was told, this was what this particular nag usually did, because she suffered from hunger pangs.

Our expeditions to the riding school had something more of interest to follow. On the way home we liked to stop at a café in Winton which I believe was called 'The Coffee Pot'. Here, jolly and quite cheap food was served and I would choose sausage and mash because we did not have such food at home. (My mother didn't believe in serving up ready mixed foods because she said that you never knew what was in them.)

But this was not the real excitement – the café was bulging full of American G.I.s (General Issue, what a horrible term!) most of whom were black and we had grown up without seeing black people except in films, so naturally we were intrigued. Fortunately, these Americans ignored us.

It was rumoured that the first batches of Americans thrown into the European conflict were prisoners, released on condition that they would join the army, black men and conscripts. I seriously doubt whether the story was true, but Americans at this time were still largely racist and there was little mixing between black and white people even in the army.

The rumours were probably false but there were bound to be some rotten apples in the vast number of men billeted in Bournemouth for a short time before being sent to Europe.

I suffered from the reality of this concept, unfortunately. One day about midday, after I had cycled home from a game of tennis, I entered our garden by means of the gate on the sea front. Now this gate, we considered, had a secret latch and our friends were unable to open it unless they knew the secret: the hand had to be inserted through a small hole and then a catch sought for under a square mount and then a small lever raised at the time that the other hand was opening the gate. Quite enough, I would have thought, to deter a hopeful intruder for some time, but I had just put my bike in the shed and gone a short way up the garden path and was out of view of people on the cliff front, when an American G.I. rushed up and tried to kiss and cuddle me. Although quite small, I was fairly strong and I struggled and kicked until I managed to get loose (maybe I kicked hard enough in the right place). Then, of course, I ran as fast as my legs would carry me into the house by the French windows, which were fortunately open and locked them behind me.

It was weeks before I dared to go out by the garden gate on my own. I thought the back door, which opened into another road, was probably safe. Strangely enough, I never told my parents or even my sisters, possibly thinking subconsciously that my freedom would be curtailed. However, every night for a long time, when I went to bed, I looked underneath it and examined the wardrobe carefully.

Although fighting for the same cause, there was some measure of dissention between our soldiers and the American G.I.s. Our boys would chant, "Overpaid, oversexed and over here!" and there was a certain amount of jealousy particularly over girls, because their abundance of dollars enabled the G.I.s to give the girls a better time. There were some fights in Bournemouth but, as there were not many British soldiers in the immediate area, the incidents were few and far between. There was also some envy of the good food that the American soldiers had. I have kept a menu for an American officer's dinner, which even today makes my mouth water. Naturally, the G.I.s did not have such sumptuous meals and, of course, there was a certain amount of grumbling on the part of the ordinary soldier, but I think that if British army menus had been enforced on the Americans, there would have been riots.

As we got nearer and nearer to D. Day the number of American soldiers congregating in the area increased vastly and every piece of large waste ground was set up as an army camp. Of course, we did not know what was going on, as the civilian population was kept in the dark about such matters, but we were not stupid and we guessed that invasion plans were afoot, but we had no inkling of when or where.

There was a large camp at the back of our school just over the railway line between Talbot Heath School and Talbot village and some of us more adventurous ones managed to get

Breakfast

Stewed Prunes

Rolled Oats in Cream   Assorted Dry Cereal

Smoked Finnan Haddie in Cream

Fried, Scrambled & Boiled Eggs

Saute Potatoes

Breakfast Bacon   Grilled Ham

Bread   Currant Scones   Toast

Tea   Cocoa   Coffee

Luncheon

Grapefruit Cocktail   Celery
Mixed Olives   Relish

Pea Soup

Fried Filet of Haddock a l'Orly

Boiled Pigs Knuckle and Sauerkraut

Welsh Rarebit (To order)

Veal Cutlet, Dish Gravy

Lima Beans

Boiled and French Fried Potatoes

Assorted Cold Cuts

Combination Salad, French Dressing

Cocoanut Pudding   Ice Cream

Edam and Camembert Cheese with Crackers

Dinner

Celery en Branch   Dill Pickles

Mixed Olives

Consomme Princesse

Saute Butterfish, Meuniere

Hungarian Veal Goulash with Noodles

Broiled Steak, Smothered Onions (Filet Mignon)

Garden Peas   Stewed Tomatoes
Baked in Jacket Potatoes

Asparagus Salad, Vinaigrette Sauce

Compote of Mixed Fruit   Chocolate Cake

American and Pimento Cheese with Crackers

Coffee   Tea

American Officers' menus, Saturday 21st October 1944

115

out of the school grounds (I don't remember how), cross the line by means of a footbridge and find ourselves in the American Army camp. The soldiers were extremely friendly and gave us bars of chocolate and they seemed to be interested in what we were studying – most of them were only just out of school themselves.

It so happened that one of our little gang had a geometry book with her, which she showed to some of the G.I.s who generally passed it around. With the arrival of chocolate and the knowledge that if we lingered long, we would probably get caught and expelled on the spot, the text book was completely forgotten. Safely back in our classroom, the missing book was immediately noted and we were certain we would be found out when some kind American handed it to our headmistress.

The relief, when we discovered a few days later that, mysteriously, the Geometry book with the owner's name on it was back in our classroom and then we realised that there were other little parties making forays into the camp to collect their bars of chocolate.

****

It was about this time whilst I was meeting highly intelligent and knowledgeable young Canadians and Americans, that I became aware of my insufficiency in these quarters and I resolved to stop messing about in lessons and take my studies more seriously and then I began to appreciate much of the school work that we were doing. At about this time, I moved up into the Sixth Form and once my fears of being made a prefect were allayed by joining the company of the few who were not elevated to that position, I soon settled in.

My voluntary work, my studies and sport kept me quite busy and, to my later regret, I didn't have much time to visit my aunt on the farm, so unfortunately she was left on her own at many weekends. One might consider her one of the unsung casualties of war. Without a car and no other means of transport available, terrified of even walking out of her small holding at night and surrounded on one side by a vast American Army camp and on the other by a firing range, she could not have felt more isolated. True, she could make phone calls, but that was not going to fill her weekends, and so, I am afraid, she took to the bottle and my mother would tell us of numerous strange falls that she had experienced in her bungalow. It did not occur to my parents that she was becoming an alcoholic and five or so years later, she tragically died from cirrhosis of the liver.

****

Then, almost suddenly, it seemed that the whole American army congregated on the cliff tops and the roads adjoining and parallel, in a few days were gone and although more Americans appeared, they were not in such numbers. Mainly they were awaiting posting to the continent and so stayed only a short time. After the 'Army of the Cliffs' had disappeared, we heard the great news that the invasion of Europe had begun. But the news on the days following was tinged with sadness when we heard of the great losses suffered by the allied forces and particularly the Americans whose landings on the beaches had not come completely as a surprise to the Germans. At that time, our propaganda was such that we heard little of the tragedies but much of the successes, the object being to keep up the morale of the civilian population. However, in spite of set backs, our armies were forging ahead but now the Germans were fighting for their homeland with their backs to the wall. Their numbers had been considerably depleted by their war of attrition in Russia but they were not prepared to give in.

The Germans had a secret weapon with which they hoped to secure victory, namely the V-1 or doodlebug. These were bombs with wings that they launched from ramps on sites on the French coast and, of course, they required no planes and airmen. Fortunately, as our invasion armies progressed along the French coast these launching sites were captured and, in Bournemouth, we never received these terrifying missiles as they had a comparatively short range and were largely targeted on London.

When my father heard about these doodlebugs, he recalled a composition that I had written in 1940 when we were still studying with our governess, Miss Ford. Naturally he had been interested in our education and he had kept my exercise book entitled English Compositions and so he hunted around and eventually ferreted out the old exercise book and quickly found an essay entitled 'My Inventions'. I must explain that our governess had previously asked us to write on what we wanted to be when we grew up, and I had declared in youthful enthusiasm that I wanted to be an inventor.

Quite logically, Miss Ford's next request was an essay on inventions and so, it came about that I wrote concerning an unmanned, targeted bomb that could be sent to blitz Berlin, which was much on the lines of the doodlebugs that were now being delivered on London. One of the major differences was that my fearsome weapon had to be taken to a great height to be launched. I even included a primitive drawing of this fearsome weapon and went on to invent a fantastic antidote if the Germans should retaliate. Luckily, on the next page, I had confessed that I was no scientist.

I vaguely remembered it, but had long since discarded my ambitions to be an inventor having gone through a whole gamut of occupational aspirations. In those days, not many girls had career ambitions and we, and many of our female friends, were brought up to be good housewives and mothers.

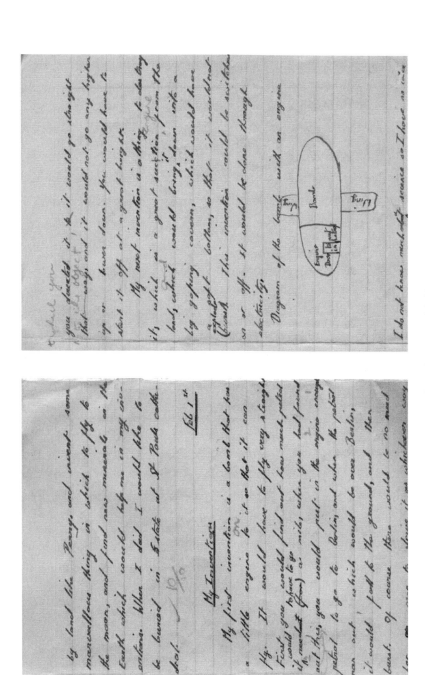

Feb 1st

My Inventions

My first invention is a boat that can fly very straight and a little engine on it so that it can fly. It would have to fly very straight. First you could find out how much petrol it would want before to go (meant) a mile, when you had found out then you could put in the engine enough petrol to go to London and when the petrol ran out, which would to ever Boston, then it would fall to the ground, and then burst. Of course there would be no need to throw it up because it would go

by boat like Penny and meant some marvellous thing in which to fly to the moon, and find new minerals on the Earth which would help me in my inventions. When I did I would like to be buried in Estate at St Pauls cathedral.

up what you steadied it, & it would go straight that ways and it would not go very higher go or turn down. You would have to start it off at a good height.

My next invention is a thing to destroy (it), which is a great suction from the boat, which would bring down into a big getting room, which would have (light) buttons so that it worked on or off. It would be done through electricity.

Diagram of the boat with an engine.

I do not know much attack science so I have no idea.

'My Inventions' essay, 1940

119

In addition, there were not many career opportunities for girls – lady lawyers, doctors, company directors, politicians, scientists etc. were extremely rare and it was often said that if you were a 'blue stocking' no man would want to marry you. But, I digress – my father having eventually discovered my childish scribblings, promptly sent them off to the *Bournemouth Echo* and then to the *Daily Mirror*, both of which papers, I believe, printed them. For your amusement, I have included a copy of these scribblings.

The V-1 bombs were particularly nasty because there was no air raid warning with its resultant scramble to the nearest air raid shelter, and the bombs could be sent any time of the night or the day with impunity. It was said that if you heard them coming and then the engine cut out you were safe, but if you heard nothing then you might be the target for that bomb, so fear was present every minute of one's life. It was really quite logical that nothing would be heard if you happened to be the target. These nasty fellows glided down silently and the engine noise was too far distant to be heard when the glide began. Naturally, these abominable machines were called pilotless planes and there was a famous cartoon of the time showing a 'planeless pilot'. Perhaps it is a feature of British society that it can find mirth in adversity and maybe that was one of the reasons that the Nazi war machine was not able to destroy the British morale.

Why were these doodlebugs called V-1s? The reason, needless to say, was that the Germans were about to launch an even more sinister weapon, namely V-2. This had similarities with the first V bomb but it was bigger and better, as far as the Germans were concerned, and the thought of them was much more terrifying to us. They did not have to have launching pads so they could continue to spread death and destruction after the French coastal launching pads had been dismantled. They were rocket propelled and did not rely on fuel for their journey once they had been launched and consequently their range was considerably greater than the V-1s. In fact, had not the allied advance been fairly rapid, they would have extended their range to most of England. As far as the residents of Bournemouth were concerned, we had a lucky escape. A V-1 landed in the New Forest and one or two V-2s were rumoured to have landed in Winchester.

****

Although most of the Americans had left our shores, there were still Canadian and Australian airmen coming and going in Bournemouth, so our visits to the Knights of St Columbus canteen and the White Hermitage continued as did our entertaining many airmen at our home, kind courtesy of my mother. Sometimes, when time permitted, we were able to show these visitors from far away places some of the beauties of the surrounding countryside. I remember a particular airman who borrowed my father's bicycle to go on an expedition out to the edge of the New Forest. He was obviously quite an experienced cyclist, but nevertheless rode straight into a gorse bush which had us all laughing helplessly. It seemed that he had never been on a bicycle that had hand brakes and his only method of stopping was by back peddling which, on my father's bike, had no effect at all. On the other hand, we had no knowledge of bikes without hand brakes so it had been impossible to warn him.

Another day, in late autumn, I took a young Canadian on the bus to Salisbury, a city that always delighted me. He was much impressed with the Cathedral and the ancient houses and inns, but then he wished to see Stonehenge about which I knew very little except that it was a pile of ancient stones in a bleak spot and it was quite a cold day. But the fame of Stonehenge had obviously spread well beyond our shores and so I consented to finding another bus that would take us somewhere near.

When we arrived at the venerable stones there was not another soul in the world on that wind-blasted plain. We wandered amongst the vast rocks and my Canadian friend was quite moved. Unfortunately, in my stupid ignorance, I could tell him nothing about these prehistoric rocks concerning which he was much better informed than I was. The expected return of the bus to Salisbury allowed us plenty of time to speculate on the origins and meaning of Stonehenge, but I must admit that I had a longing to clamber into the comparative comfort of a draughty bus away from a wintry blast on a wind swept, open plain.

Stonehenge

The Americans seemed to have deserted Bournemouth and we were sad to see them depart because on the whole we had got on with them extremely well. Maybe that was because of a little booklet that they had all been given by the American authorities telling them how to make friends with the British. We laughed and laughed when we read some of it, because, being written by Americans, it considered as undesirable, matters that would not offend the average Englishman. I remember the first recommendation in the booklet declared that the soldiers were not to say that our trains were small, neither should they comment that British houses were wee or cute. Probably one suggestion was that they should not show the pamphlet to British people, because I saw only one copy, or maybe they threw their instructions away when they discovered that we were not so reserved and that we did discuss matters other than the weather. It seemed that the Americans reciprocated and appreciated our friendship. After the war, I learnt that the American 78th Division, which was quartered in Bournemouth, published in their Association magazine such comments as, 'How nice the people of Bournemouth were' and 'even inviting us to tea and serving desserts that they had sacrificed from their rations'.

****

As far as the war in Europe was concerned, the Western Allies were progressing well and once the Rhine had been crossed there were signs of hope that the war in this theatre might soon be over. The Russians were forging ahead on their way to Berlin; the Allies pushed into Italy and into Western Germany and in late April linked with up the Russians forces. A few days later both Hitler and Goebbels committed suicide. The end was in sight and the British at home were looking out their flags and bunting for the great day.

On several occasions, I had had the enjoyment of staying with my school friend in Weybridge, who lived in a gorgeous rambling old rectory. On these visits, I first enjoyed the delights of drinking milk shakes in a milk bar and accompanying my friend to innumerable houses in the district. Liz, as the Rector's daughter, seemed to know everyone and was most welcome in their homes.

It so happened that I was in Weybridge when the longed for V.E. Day (Victory in Europe Day, May 8th 1945) arrived and by coincidence we had arranged to see a musical play in London. I remember little about the show, possibly because of my state of euphoria over the defeat of the Nazis, but I do remember one hauntingly beautiful melody, *We'll Gather Lilacs*, which seemed most appropriate to the occasion. When we came out the celebrations were still going on but largely elsewhere in London. Unfortunately, all we saw was the seamy side of the swinging party centred on London. To my infinite disgust, we saw quite a number of utterly drunk people lying in gutters vomiting and, in my, I suppose, sheltered life, I had never seen women reeling around in drunken stupors in public. This all disgusted me so much that I vowed there and then that I would never over drink and my poor aunt's later experience reinforced this determination not to succumb to 'the bottle'.

However, the war was by no means over. We, on the Home Front, were relieved of the dangers of war, but atrociously bloody battles were still being waged on the other side of the world.

Victory

We were overjoyed to be free of bombing but we knew that the vicious war in the Far East was a long way from completion. The Japanese had brought the Americans into the war in 1941 by treacherously attacking the U.S.A. navy in Pearl Harbour on Hawaii. Following this act of perfidy, the Japanese rapidly fanned out and seemed to invade everything in the Far East and many of these lands were part of the British Commonwealth. They even threatened India.

Many British citizens were taken prisoner and suffered atrocious conditions and although we heard the news about the astoundingly fast progress that the Japanese armies were making to overrun the Far East and the Pacific islands, it was all so far away and difficult to follow partly owing to the strange names of many of the places. However, we did follow the amazing exploits of General Wingate in Burma who was the leader of the Chindits, because he had some connection with our school and in fact, we frequently prayed for his safety. Even this small theatre of the war was difficult to follow as often there was no news of him and his army while they were deep in the Burmese jungle – the Chindits were sometimes called the 'Lost Army' and were a mixed brigade of British, Gurkha and Burmese guerrillas supplied by air and thus able to fight in dense jungle behind the enemy lines. Their heroism and endurance had no bounds and we listened avidly when our headmistress could give us some news of them. We were devastated by the news of the loss of many of our Royal Navy ships with huge losses of life.

Back home, some lessening of war restrictions occurred and holidaymakers began to return as the beaches became available and some hotels and guesthouses opened up. The Americans had gone but there were still airforce men foregathering in Bournemouth awaiting posting and, in addition, there were administrative personnel proceeding to wind up matters in the locality.

For a short space of time, we had a new influx of airmen, namely emaciated prisoners of war returning from the German prisoner of war camps. These men, who had suffered hell, were a very sorry sight and they were housed for a few weeks in Bournemouth before returning to their loved ones. They received medical attention and an extremely careful food regime to restore them to health before they were able to return to their homes and their air force stations to be de-mobbed. It was essential to introduce these ex-prisoners of war to extremely small amounts of simple food very gradually, otherwise they experienced medical problems such as appendicitis and ulcers. It must be remembered that, as prisoners, they had been almost starved and some of them had even resorted to eating grass and weeds that grew on the edges of their camps. Red Cross food parcels rarely reached them and some of them suffered from psychological problems. We met quite a number of them, but although we would have been most interested to hear of their experiences, few of them volunteered any information and we were tactful enough not to make enquiries.

Rationing remained as stringent as ever and there seemed to be an even greater shortage of all consumer goods. At this time I had taken on a sudden growing spurt and, as my sisters had stopped growing for some time, there were no 'hand ons'. I seemed to be almost devoid of clothes. My mother in her wisdom, when we reached the age of 16, gave us an allowance so that we began to understand the management of money. This allowance of 15 shillings (75p) a week, which to the modern reader must seem miniscule, was in fact quite generous. Rationing, the points system and clothes coupons all ensured that prices remained stable and it was only people dealing in the black market, in order to obtain more than their fair share of goods, who paid astronomical prices.

To put matters in their right perspective: pre-war, my mother paid a live-in young domestic help 15 shillings a week, rising to 30 shillings at the age of 21 and there was virtually no inflation during the war. My great needs in the realm of clothes were dictated by clothes coupons as well as money, and in the summer I was tempted into buying two pairs of attractive sandals largely because I could not make up my mind which pair I liked the best. Having no more clothes coupons left, I had to wear these flimsy sandals all through the year. I suffered cold feet all the next winter and when my mother suggested that my feet might be cold, I am afraid I told a little lie and assured her that they were quite comfortable just in case I was rebuked for not buying sensible shoes.

I managed to survive on the meagre allowance of clothes permitted, as I was not particularly interested in dress, but my more dress conscious sisters went to considerable lengths to dress smartly. They traded in coupons (a ration of sugar or tea to an elderly relation bought quite a number of clothing coupons and was perfectly legal). They rushed to the dressmaker with an outmoded dress to make it into a fashionable skirt and they even made home alterations using a new sewing machine that my mother had managed to buy for this purpose.

Americans sometimes gave us nylon stockings, which were unheard of on the British domestic market. Nylon had recently been invented in the U.S.A. and proved to be an extremely strong fibre and the first stockings did not seem to ladder, so that two pairs of nylons gave me at least two year's wear. Needless to say, I coddled them well and only wore them when I was going out in the evening. The rest of the time, I went bare legged as most young girls did but I wore socks at school.

Being not over-interested in clothes, much of my allowance was spent on books, which did not seem to be limited in number although the quality was somewhat downmarket. The paper was poor and the quality of the covers of hardbacks was indifferent. Paperbacks did exist but they were not as prolific as they are today.

For a number of Christmases my Aunt had kindly bought me a membership of a book library at Brights Departmental Store in the Arcade and this sufficed for most of my fictional reading. I would rush down practically every day in the holidays just before the shop closed to exchange books. However, there were many non-fiction books I desired and I had to buy these out of my allowance.

You may wonder why I didn't use the public library and you will be amused by my answer - my mother and father were quite convinced that we would catch germs from some of the books lent out and I must admit that some of the ones my friends had borrowed looked pretty tacky, much dog-eared and stained with remains of meals and drink. They probably were expected to last longer in order to help the war effort!

****

It was soon after V.E. Day that I decided to leave school and, as they say 'move on'. My mother was delighted, because she hoped that I would be her companion and helpmate until I found a suitable husband and settled down to 'domestic bliss' and raising a family. I am afraid I disappointed her and went on to college.

Leaving school, in theory sounded nice, but when the day came for departure, it was quite traumatic. I had enjoyed my time at Talbot Heath and made some wonderful friends whom thankfully I still see to this day. Then, in addition, we couldn't have asked for a more superb environment in which to study and play. The school was new, designed by well-known architects and purpose built. In fact it wasn't quite completed in 1942. My mother and father had been invited to attend the official opening in 1935 and had been particularly impressed by the fine architecture and particularly that of the boarding houses. As for the grounds, there was a wide extent of heath and woodland and we only had to cross Rothesay Road to be in the most expansive playing fields: tennis (hard and grass), hockey and cricket and plenty of room for other activities. There were many traditions well established because the school had quite a history before it moved to Talbot Heath.

Talbot Heath School, St Mary's Boarding House

One tradition that really stands out in my memory occurred annually on the school's birthday when the whole school congregated in the hall and a short service held. When we came to a certain hymn the first verse was sung and then form by

129

form we filed out into the quadrangle continuing singing. The more senior forms came last and these were in the balcony; we had quite a stretch to cover including a stairway. It was with great delight that when we entered the quadrangle we found that we were singing the same word as those already gathered there. So it was with almost overwhelming sadness that I began the school summer holidays.

In July and August, the news from the Far East was still pretty grim, but the Allied forces were beginning to get the upper hand. However, we knew that there was much horrific fighting to be done before lands and particularly Pacific Islands were restored.

Japan was a great warrior nation and their faith made them believe that it was good to die for their country, so there were many kamikaze exponents particularly amongst Japanese pilots who loaded their planes with bombs and in a suicide dive directed their planes straight at the target.

Then on August 6th, much to the amazement of the general public, the Americans dropped an atomic bomb on Hiroshima and devastated that large city. We had some knowledge that there was a race to create an atomic bomb between Germany and the U.S.A. because we had heard of the production of 'heavy water' in occupied Norway and the attack that had delayed the Germans in their aim to produce an atomic bomb. It was all completely new technology which we did not understand but we had rumours that something very secret was brewing in America. It seems awful now to admit that we were overjoyed with the news and we thought that the Japanese would surrender immediately.

However, the Japanese fighting spirit was not diminished and they refused to submit in spite of leaflets being dropped by American planes stating other cities would be subjected to the full horror of atomic bombs and so a second atomic bomb was released on Nagasaki. At last the Japanese made overtures to end the war and in all the allied countries there was great rejoicing and of course celebration.

****

I shall never forget the great time we all had on V.J. night (Victory over Japan, 15th August 1945). For me, it began with an impromptu dance at the West Hants Tennis Club. There I met a charming young English man with whom I danced most of the evening. He was with a group of other Bournemouth people, one of whom had a small car. When the dance finished at midnight, about half a dozen of us tried to squeeze into this little car – there just wasn't room for us all, so a couple of us clambered on the roof. The driver, when he approached the first roundabout, decided to give the upper passengers a thrill, so we circled round and round this minute roundabout clinging on for dear life (maybe the driver wanted to get rid of his extra passengers) until we were utterly dizzy.

At last our driver decided to steer his car to the beach west of the pier where some of the party went for a post midnight swim. I didn't take part in this escapade. I had never swum in the dark and I didn't like the look of inky black water just seeming like thick sticky oil; neither was I accustomed to swimming in my birthday suit. Then too, I had more respect for my clothes coupons.

Eventually my friend of the evening walked me home. We didn't receive a pleasant welcome in spite of my escort beginning the conversation with apologies for keeping me out late. To give my mother her due, she had been decidedly worried so she burst out with queries such as, "Where have you been at this time of night?" and, "What have you been doing all this time?" and finally the bold statement, "We have phoned the police."

It had never occurred to me that my parents would not understand that most of the youth of Bournemouth had gone completely mad celebrating the end of the fighting. It was as if a great blanket had been smothering us and, at last, it had been taken away.

What happened to my charming escort of the evening? I never saw him again. I think that he was terrified by the thought of meeting my irate parents again and so, he became for me, yet one more of 'the ships that pass in the night' which wartime produces and which we care to store in our memories.

"For now my song is ended"